THE 60-MINUTE COOKBOOK

The
60-Minute Cookbook

by
PAMELA WESTLAND

FABER AND FABER
London & Boston

First published in 1980
by Faber and Faber Limited
3 Queen Square London WC1N 3AU
First published in Faber Paperbacks in 1981
Set, printed and bound in Great Britain by
Fakenham Press Limited
Fakenham Norfolk

British Library Cataloguing in Publication Data

Westland, Pamela
The 60-minute cookbook
1. Cookery
I. Title   II. Sixty-minute cookbook
641.5'55   TX652

ISBN 0–571–11554–3

CONTENTS

COLOUR PLATES

ACKNOWLEDGEMENTS

The author and the publishers are grateful to the following firms and organizations who supplied or sponsored photographs:

THE HOME BAKING BUREAU (Plate 1); MATTESSONS MEATS (Plate 2); CARMEL PRODUCE (Plate 4); THE PASTA INFORMATION CENTRE (Plate 5); BACOFOIL LTD (Plate 6); THE BRITISH BACON BUREAU (Plate 7); BRITISH MEAT (Plate 8); JIF LEMON (Plate 8); GALE'S HONEY (Plate 9)

They are also grateful to the firms who supplied items of kitchen equipment illustrated in Plate 3:

BRABANTIA (UK) LTD: apple corer, cheese grater, garlic press, potato chipper

KITCHEN DEVILS: knives and knife sharpener, scissors, potato peeler, knife rack

LE CREUSET: red enamelled cast-iron casserole

NUTBROWN HOUSEWARES: egg slicer, egg wedger, grapefruit knife, spatulas, superslicer, tomato slicer

PRESTIGE GROUP LTD: wall can opener; (Skyline): fruit and vegetable baller, non-stick bakeware, swivel-bladed potato peeler, vegetable brush

PEARSONS OF CHESTERFIELD: round brown glazed casserole

SALTER HOUSEWARES LTD: cook's brush, Easislice De Luxe, Weighmix

SUNBEAM ELECTRIC LTD: Multi Cooker

TOWER HOUSEWARES LTD: three Tower Royale pans

METAL BOX LTD (Tala): cook's measure, egg separator, flour sifter, one-handed whisk, potato crimper, potato ricer

INTRODUCTION

The 60-Minute Cookbook—what does it mean? My terms of reference were to present recipes that any cook would be proud to serve at lunch or dinner for six, and yet be able to prepare in under an hour. I have not assumed that every household has a freezer, nor that the cook in a hurry will want to make too much use of canned and other convenience foods.

It is for all those people who, like myself, love to cook interesting food, yet never seem to have enough time. It is for those days when, on the spur of the moment, you have invited friends to a meal knowing that, with luck, you may have barely thirty minutes at home before they arrive. For the occasions when you have to squash the preparation for a meal the next day into what time is left late one evening or early one morning. For the times when people are staying and you want to enjoy their company, a drink at the pub, or the sun in the garden, with the rest of the family. No one wants to emerge from the kitchen like a hermit, just in time to sound the gong for the next meal. And no one should have to.

The recipes are divided into three main sections: first courses, main dishes, with a comprehensive selection of accompaniments, and puddings. Each section is then divided into dishes that can be cooked on the spot starting from scratch, just before the meal is to be served; those that, with a little forethought, can be partially prepared in advance, the night or morning before, and those that rely heavily on quickly-prepared ingredients from the store-cupboard.

With careful selection from these recipes, it should be possible to compile a three-course menu that could be prepared from start to finish in under an hour, allowing extra time for the main dish to be cooking while people linger over drinks and the starter, and for the pudding to be cooking or cooling while the main course is in progress. But take heart! In very tight time-schedules, it should not be necessary to cook all three courses. Understanding family and friends would be off to a perfectly good start with something delicious, like pâté or a selection of Continental sausages, from the delicatessen, or come to a happy conclusion with a bowl of fresh fruit and an interesting cheese. Prepare the main course and one other in the time limit and you can take a bow.

The actual amount of time you spend in preparing a meal depends to a large extent on two things: your own personal sleight of hand, and the appliances and gadgets you have to help you. As more and more of us seem to live in a constant whirl, we are gradually moving further towards a fully-automated kitchen. Yet I have not assumed that all readers have a push-button kitchen at their command. That would be too easy: and cheating.

In the first section, Slick Operators, I have enlarged on a list of the time-savers I have built up gradually and with some care (since money as well as time is a consideration), and have now come to rely on. The list probably shows that I am an old-fashioned cook at heart, who has come somewhat reluctantly, yet gratefully, to accept the helping hand offered by high-speed gadgets. Next, in Fast Methods, I have given a few basic step-by-step guides to some of the jobs—chopping, slicing, cutting—that, if we are to be fast cooks, have to become almost a reflex action, with or without special equipment. At the end of this section, A Fast Set-up gives hints on setting a table at fast and furious speed, and conjuring up pretty decorations when flowers are out of the question. Then, in Always in Store, suggestions for the type of ingredients I find it useful to have in reserve. Following the main recipe sections a further section is by way of insurance. Called Finishing Touches, it is a home-made store-cupboard of sauces, dressings, toppings and garnishes to prepare on a calm day and produce with a flourish on a hectic one.

1

SLICK OPERATORS

Not so very long ago—at least, it was after I had written and tested the recipes for three cookery books—a manufacturer asked me which make of electric mixer I used. To his enormous surprise I replied quite truthfully, 'A wooden spoon and a fork.' So I make no claim to be kitchen gadget mad.

To be honest, I had been rather sceptical about so many of the kitchen aids that shower the market now. But gradually over the years I have been converted, and have built up a small battery of tools and appliances that really are worth their weight in gold to me. Some of them have proved so useful, I wonder how I ever managed without them.

Obviously, any such collection is as individual to each of us as a range of cosmetics or a selection of perfumes would be. We all react in different ways to various jobs, and are each bound to find more or less useful the various aids at our disposal. You have only to watch two people peeling potatoes to know that one can do in a twinkling something the other sees as a major chore.

One other thing. I believe it is vital to be able to accept at least a degree of untidiness in a kitchen that is to be a really speedy-food scene. If everything is neatly and tidily put away in drawers and cupboards, the owner will no doubt know a glow of pride as she surveys the barren expanse, but a moment of near-panic when she is faced with a tough mealtime deadline. I sometimes despair when I look round my kitchen, at the big earthenware jars of wooden spoons, kitchen tools and gadgets; electric toaster, electric mixer, weighing scales, recipe books, food slicer, salt box and pepper mill ranged along the working surfaces; knife racks, foil and paper rolls and spice jars on the wall; plates, dishes, cups and saucers, flour bins and storage jars on open shelves; and the bulging rows of pots, pans, casseroles, chicken and fish bricks on top of the wall cupboards. But at least I know that I'm under starter's orders when I need to go into action.

Knives

I put these first for there is no doubt at all that a selection of the correct knives for the various kitchen tasks is the best possible investment any cook can have. A poor quality knife, one not properly designed for the job in hand, or one not properly sharpened can waste more time and temper than anything.

Basically, there are three types of edges: a straight, smooth edge; a scalloped or wavy edge, and a serrated edge. The type of edge affects the suitability of the knife to a particular task, but not its quality. The same quality of cutler's steel can be given any of those finishes.

There is a certain amount of overlap in the performance of knives with the three types of edges, and to an extent the choice of one over the other may be a matter of personal preference. The following notes are general guidelines.

STRAIGHT EDGE

Knives with a straight edge are the cutlery version of the old-fashioned cut-throat razor. Think of them as a guillotine, rather than a saw. They are for all the activities when a forward cutting motion is used—for dicing, chopping, shredding, paring and peeling. Some people prefer straight-edged knives also for cutting and carving meat and poultry. Specialist knives with a straight edge include peelers, parers, vegetable knives, carvers and slicers.

Some makes of straight-edged knives have what is called a hollow-ground finish. This means that the blade is scooped out to a certain depth before the final super-sharp cutting edge is ground on.

SCALLOPED EDGE

Knives with a scalloped edge may be considered as the cutlery version of a carpenter's saw—at least, a saw with very large teeth. The smooth, even curves along the edge give the blade 'grip' which makes the first cut into, say, a crusty loaf or a tomato skin a good deal easier than it is with a straight-edged blade.

Both scalloped and serrated edges are used for slicing backwards and forwards, to and fro like a saw. Special-purpose knives with scalloped edges include meat and bread knives, roast meat slicers, carvers, frozen food knives, and because they are so versatile, those referred to as cook's knives and all-purpose knives.

It is a mistake to think that blades with a scalloped edge should not be sharpened: they should. There are notes on sharpening knives at the end of this section.

SERRATED EDGE

The ridged edges given to modern knives are the equivalent of the roughness that was a feature of cutting edges kept keen on a whetstone or grindstone.

Serrated knives are particularly useful for the preparation of salads. They, too, take in their stride the first cut into tomato skin, and are good for slicing lemons, oranges and (with a curved blade) preparing grapefruit.

Serrated edges may not need sharpening for months or even years, but eventually they will.

I use the Kitchen Devil range of surgical steel knives (so called because the steel is the same quality as that used for surgical scalpels). Both black and white polypropylene handles are dishwasher-proof—another good factor, time-wise. The range includes straight, scalloped and serrated-edged knives and the following seven are the ones I use most:

Cook's knife has a scalloped-edged blade 15·2-cm (6-in) long with a curved, serrated tip. This copes with all cutting up, boning and filleting of meat and fish.

Five-way peeler-parer, with an adjustable guard to guide the blade for thick and thin slices; it can be used either right- or left-handed.

Kitchen knife with a 11·4-cm (4½-in) blade which, because of its minute serrations, deals quickly with all fruit and vegetable slicing.

Meat and bread knife with a 20-cm (8-in) scalloped blade.

Roast super-slicer with unusually deep scallops on one side of the 19·7-cm (7¾-in) blade and tooth-like serrations on the other.

Salad knife with a 11·1-cm (4⅜-in) blade with serrations right along one of the twin serving prongs. It's spectacular for slicing oranges and lemons and poking out the pips, useful for work at the bar, too.

Vegetable knife with a 6-cm (2½-in) straight-edged blade, is an ideal 'chopper' which copes easily with all but the largest vegetables.

CLEAVERS

Chinese cooks use a cleaver-knife to cut and chop meat and vegetables. When these are used skilfully—and this means rhythmically—they really make short work of it. They are obtainable in most kitchen-ware shops now, and it is worth considering investing in one. (See page 24 for method.)

SHARPENING KNIVES

Unless you keep the sharpest possible cutting edge on all your knives you are throwing time away. Most experts agree that the best tool for the job is a butcher's steel. But since it is important to hold a knife blade at exactly the right angle against the steel—the angle at which the cutting edge is ground—many people find it more reassuring to use a knife sharpener. There are various types, among them one with a rotary wheel action, and another which consists of a pair of crossed steels.

To sharpen a knife with a butcher's steel, hold the steel in your left hand, horizontal and parallel to your body, at about hip height. Hold hollow-ground knife blades at an angle of 25°, others at 45°, to the steel and, using rhythmic movements, stroke the blade to the very tip across the steel, first on the top and then on the underside. Sharpen serrated edges on the smooth side only.

Knives with scalloped or serrated edges are slightly more vulnerable to damage than straight-edged ones, since the protrusions are easily 'burred' when they come into contact with, say, a carving fork, and need constantly 'touching up' on a steel. Purists recommend that the knives are touched up on a steel both before and after use.

Other Kitchen Tools and Equipment

If you have a good range of kitchen knives and, perhaps, some of the electrical equipment discussed on pages 21–23, you will not need many other gadgets. But there are certain jobs done in such small amounts that a hand tool is just as quick. Here are some of the types of equipment and the gadgets I use most.

APPLE CORER

If you are cutting an apple into eight slices and you don't use a corer, that's eight times you have to scoop out the pips. The

Photograph: Fred Mancini

3. Non-stick pans and bakeware, razor-sharp knives, non-slip bowls, quick
time.

Photograph: The Home Baking Bureau

1. A selection of fresh and fragrant breads to accompany soups, salads, pâtés, mousses and cheese.

2. Sliced in moments, spicy continental sausages get a meal off to a tasty, good-looking start.

Photograph: Mattessons Meats

Brabantia corer has an unusually sharp cutting edge and a good depth—8·5 cm (3½ in)—that takes the complete core of a large apple. I find mine useful to make quick decorations from a block of butter, scooping out neat little cylinders, or tiny pastry circles to overlap round the edge of a pie.

BAKEWARE

Surely no other single invention saves more time and trouble in the kitchen than non-stick surfaces. From the preparation stage, when one used to have to grease pans, right through to the washing up, I send thought-waves of gratitude to the scientist who invented the stick-resistant finishes. I am gradually replacing everything as fast as I justifiably can, from roasting tins to baking sheets, with a new range of non-stick cooking ware. The only exception is a set of French flan dishes, shiny bright and crinkled at the edges, with push-out bases. They make the most professional-looking quiches possible and I haven't so far found any non-stick ones nearly as good.

CAN OPENER

For all those times when we are grateful for canned food, it is important not to waste a moment actually opening the can. I find a wall model quickest and easiest to use.

COOK'S BRUSH

You are just about to serve a dish and you notice little pools of oil or fat floating to the top. Whisk them away with a Salter cook's brush. It is a thick, light and airy bunch of soft fibres, sparkling white on a plastic handle. You just brush or dip it over a casserole, gravy, sauce or soup and the fat immediately runs straight up the fibres, like magic. It's very easy to wash, too.

COOK'S MEASURE

Quick reference for metric, Imperial and cup measurements (American and British), particularly invaluable when following American recipes, is simple with a Tala measure.

EGG SEPARATOR

Most people can crack an egg on the side of a bowl and have it perfectly separated every time. For anyone who can't, a Tala egg separator eliminates the uncertainty.

EGG SHAPERS

Hard-boiled eggs fall into thin slices or wedges with two Nutbrown gadgets. And with a sprinkling of paprika pepper, there's an instant and colourful decoration.

FLOUR SIFTER

Many brands of flour are sold ready-sifted, but sometimes you just can't avoid sifting ingredients together—and icing sugar is notorious for ganging up. A Tala sifter, like a tankard, with a handle and high straight sides, is quicker to use than a sieve—and it doesn't shower you or the kitchen with dust.

FOOD SLICER

I never thought I needed a food slicer until I had one. It's a Salter Easislice De Luxe, with stainless steel blades, a food guide for accuracy and a finger guard for safety. It means that I can buy a whole salami or garlic sausage, for example, which store like a dream, and slice off thin rounds for a first course at a moment's notice. I also use it to slice rye bread for open sandwiches, thick melon rings to pile high with other fresh fruit, green pepper rings for salads and lots of other things. The slicer does need to be kept ready assembled, where you can use it quickly.

FRUIT AND VEGETABLE BALLER

It's quicker to serve a melon in slices or wedges than to scoop it into balls. But a fruit and vegetable baller can save you time in other ways. Tiny balls of potato cook much more quickly, either by boiling or frying, than whole ones, and look much prettier too.

FRUIT ZESTER

A French gadget, called Econome, rather like a little trowel with five tiny circular holes. You draw it firmly over the peel of citrus fruit, and lo and behold, there are the thinnest, narrowest strips to decorate or flavour a dish, and not a trace of the bitter pith.

GARLIC PRESS

The Brabantia one has a particularly good feature—the grid is removable for quick and thorough washing.

GRAPEFRUIT KNIFE

Often there isn't time to peel fresh grapefruit at all, but when there is, the Nutbrown scalloped and not-too-curved blade makes short work of it. Also good for preparing melon.

KITCHEN SCISSORS

Try them in the shop, open and close them, make a few imaginary cuts with them before buying. The balance is not always right for every size and shape of hand; one make I have feels cumbersome and top heavy. I always use my Kitchen Devil scissors for stringy celery, spring onion, bacon rind and so on.

MANDOLINE SLICER

A narrow wooden board with an angled inset cutting blade, rather like an old-fashioned scrubbing board, makes paper-thin slices of carrot, cucumber, potato, celariac and cheese possible in seconds.

MIXING BOWLS, IN A RANGE OF SIZES

I like the old-fashioned pottery ones, but the material is less important than the size. If you use bowls that are too small you will spend valuable time wiping up the splashes. If they are too large, the mixing takes longer. Many cooks swear by the brightly-coloured plastic bowls with a rubber ring in the base. They neither scratch nor chip and the rubber prevents them from slipping on working surfaces.

POTATO CHIPPER

It cuts cube-section strips of raw vegetables either to save on cooking time, or to use as a garnish in minestrone soup, or as crudités with a soft pâté. You pop in the vegetable, push down the lever, and out come the strips. Mine is a Brabantia.

POTATO CRIMPER

Slice boiled potatoes into appetizing-looking crinkly slices with a Tala crimper before tossing them in hot butter and chopped parsley.

POTATO RICER

Potatoes can often be the poor relation of a meal, when all the time and thought has gone into the other components. Fortunately, my husband rightly prides himself on taking more trouble mashing potatoes, with correspondingly better results, than I do. A Tala potato ricer, like a mini perforated pan with a clamp handle, pushes mashed potato through in no time, transforming it into light, fluffy squiggles.

POTS AND PANS

As with bakeware, non-stick surfaces are invaluable. My whole kitchen has been revolutionized since I went over to the Tower Royale range of saucepans and frying-pans, and I have given away to the lucky local jumble sale every other one I owned—except my treasured old copper pan. All the Royale pans are made of thick aluminium with black enamelled bases, which absorb rather than reflect and give quick, even heat. The Silverstone non-stick finish is the most reliable I know, and absolutely nothing sticks. The steam control dial on every lid means that you can fry without splashing and simmer without risk of liquids boiling over.

SIEVES

A conical and a dish-shaped sieve are both useful for straining vegetables, sauces (especially those that go lumpy) and soups.

SPOONS

A large range of wooden spoons standing in a kitchen jar is, for me, as decorative as a bunch of flowers. And infinitely useful, for beating, stirring and positively not scratching precious pan surfaces. Add a plastic spatula to make the quickest work of scraping out mixing bowls. Nothing else is quite so pliable or fits quite so neatly round the curves.

SWIVEL-BLADED POTATO PEELER

This Skyline gadget I wouldn't part with for anything. I even take mine with me when I go to stay with friends, in case I'm asked to peel the potatoes with something not half as efficient. It has such a sharp cutting edge, such an easy action, it skims over potatoes, parsnips, apples, anything. It takes a second or two to peel a few strips of carrot for a bright garnish that can 'make' a dish. Useful, too, for finely paring lemons and oranges.

TOMATO SLICER

My Nutbrown has a fat serrated blade shaped almost to a circle at the 'tip' end, to support the tomato slices as they are cut—useful when the tomatoes are the least bit squashy.

VEGETABLE BRUSH

Perfect for washing vegetables with ridges or nooks and crannies, like celery and Jerusalem artichokes, and for whisking the skin off very new potatoes and carrots.

WEIGHING SCALES

Like most cooks, I will guess weights and measures whenever I can get away with it. But when accuracy is essential, I find the Salter Weighmix perfectly designed for speed. The large-capacity mixing bowl and the re-zero dial mean that you can add one ingredient after another, setting the dial back to 0 each time, without any error-prone mental arithmetic. In tiny kitchens, wall scales are a great space-saver.

WHISKS

I don't believe you can beat a metal balloon whisk for sauces of the béchamel type. But there are times when a one-handed whisk, by Tala, is a positive blessing. While you are pumping egg yolks up and down in a bowl with one hand, you can be holding the telephone receiver, stirring a sauce or reaching for a packet with the other. Method study at the double!

Electrical Equipment

ELECTRIC FRYING-PAN (SUNBEAM MULTI COOKER)

This is one of the most versatile pieces of kitchen equipment. I use mine for braising, small roasts, and all those party dishes, like liver in Madeira sauce or lemon veal, in which the meat is sautéed before the sauce ingredients are stirred in. And on informal occasions, it is quite a showpiece on the table.

EXPRESS COOKER AND GRILL, MOULINEX

The food is done in double quick time: it is sandwiched between two non-stick ribbed hotplates, and so cooks evenly and simultaneously on both sides. You don't have to watch for half time to turn the meat or fish as on a conventional grill—which I used to find, all too often led to wrenched-off skin or a broken backbone (on the fish, not me!) if I manhandled the trout too hastily.

Food Preparation Systems

It seems to be the ambition of every busy cook to own one of the increasing number of food preparation systems, or electric mixers which, if you achieve all the attachments, make other tools and gadgets redundant.

FOOD PROCESSORS

Most of us have a friend or a relation who is eager to introduce us to the seemingly magical properties of food processors, demonstrating the almost unbelievable speeds with which these appliances can chop, mix, blend, slice and grind ingredients. There are several models already on the market, and more being developed all the time. What they all have in common, apart from their speed and efficiency, is compactness, a vital feature for everyone with a small kitchen and hardly any space to spare. A food processor ready at hand on the working surface does the jobs of a dozen pairs of hands, and suddenly such dishes as pâté and potted meats, pastry and puddings are fast food. And just as quickly as they blend flour and fat, chop meat, grate breadcrumbs or shred vegetables, they can be washed, dried and reassembled, eager for the next task.

HAND MIXER

Even with a food processor, you still need a hand mixer, one of the most invaluable appliances invented. Use this to whisk egg whites and sponge mixtures, whip cream to its maximum volume, and beat the sauces, particularly those that are best beaten over a pan of hot water. Choose, if possible, a model that comes complete with stand, so that you do not have to idle away even the few moments it takes to perform its tasks, or a hand mixer which can hang on its own conveniently placed wall-bracket and will be always ready for use and a real time-saver.

LIQUIDIZER

Having been spoilt by the luxury of reducing fruit and vegetables to a smooth purée, and meat and fish to a smooth paste at the flick of a switch, I probably would not now bother to make such dishes at all if I had to do the work by hand—and they would in any case be out of the question on all fast-food occasions. So many of the soups, pâtés, mousses and sauces that I take for granted are entirely by courtesy of the liquidizer.

TABLE-TOP MIXER

Old habits die hard, and it took me ages to realize that the mixer really does beat cream without buttering it; makes it unnecessary, if the bowl and the beater are heated first, to whisk egg yolks and sugar over a pan of hot water, and so on. A full year after I first had the mixer, I still caught myself dismissing recipes because momentarily I would forget how rapidly it would beat and whisk and knead and stir for me. Now I admit that I am at a complete loss without my Kenwood Chef.

Colander and sieve attachment. Indispensable for the obstinately stringy foods that even a high-speed liquidizer does not reduce quite to a pulp—raspberries and celery, for example—and for sorting out the stones in such orchard fruits as plums and greengages. The words 'sieve thoroughly' in a recipe hold no terrors any more.

Mincer attachment. There are times when it is quicker to mince meat and fish and cook them in a short, sharp way, than it is to cook the ingredients whole. Unthinkable, of course, without a mincing attachment.

High-speed slicer and shredder attachment. For salads, stir-fried vegetables, cheese, nuts and chocolate, the high-speed shredder really is a slick operator. The only problem is in keeping up the pace and feeding the machine as quickly as it gobbles up the ingredients. I recently had to prepare some of the food for a charity supper for two hundred guests, and made a selection of four mixed salads, from start to finish, in three-quarters of an hour. How's that for a testimonial?

But as with all multi-purpose appliances, one cannot over-emphasize the importance of keeping the mixer and the attachments at the ready. This usually means having the mixer itself on a working surface and the various attachments immediately overhead, perhaps in a cupboard. If they are packed away in their various boxes they will be out of sight and out of mind and the effort involved in getting them out will outweigh the convenience of doing so.

2
FAST METHODS

Given the right tools for the job, and a certain deftness, there is no reason why any food preparation should be time-consuming, or a chore. If, of course, we choose to spend ages beating, kneading, mixing or chopping, that's fine; perhaps, deep down, we need that kind of therapy—or exercise. But we can certainly do without it on all those occasions when time is running out and we have to prepare a meal—fast.

There are some routine jobs, like chopping an onion or slicing meat, that just have to be done. And they are so much part and parcel of cooking that it pays to take a fresh look at them. Perhaps the methods we have been using for years—or, just as important, tools that have become old friends—are not the most effective. Maybe we could cut a minute or two off the preparation time here, another minute there; time which could then be spent in whipping up a pudding or preparing an extra vegetable. Here are a few fast-worker hints to help speed things merrily along.

Chopping and Slicing Vegetables

You must always use a wooden board for chopping, or, if you are lucky enough to have one, an old wooden chopping block. Never use a hard, non-resistant surface such as a piece of laminated plastic, marble, glass or tile—you will ruin the knife and your chances of making a good job of it. Chop to a steady rhythm, whether you use a knife or a cleaver, and stop before the board begins to 'melt', as the Chinese say. This means before you begin to add tiny wood shavings to your ingredients.

For Chinese stir-frying, it is important to slice vegetables thinly and evenly, to expose the maximum surface to the cooking oil for the minimum amount of time.

Diagonal slicing is used for hard and semi-hard vegetables such as carrots, ginger and cabbages. Irregularly-shaped vegetables are always sliced first from the narrow end, working towards the thicker one. You can use either a very sharp knife or a cleaver. In either case, the cuts should be precise and even and the cutting action quick and rhythmic.

To cut vegetables into dice it is much easier to work systematically, not to go at it haphazardly. That way results in some minute pieces and some huge chunks. To slice a carrot, for example, first cut along the length three or four times to make narrow strips. Turn the carrots over on the board 90° and cut through the length again, into another three or four strips. Then chop into dice at right angles to these cuts.

CELERY

Wash the celery stalks carefully with a brush along the grain. Running water from the tap swooshes the dirt away.

1 To cut it into small pieces, lay the stalk on a wooden board in front of you, parallel to the edge of the table.
2 Using a very sharp knife, slit once or twice through the length, to cut very fine strips.
3 Either pick up the celery carefully, holding all the strips firmly together, and snip into very small pieces, using sharp kitchen scissors, or cut through the strips with a sharp knife.

FRESH HERBS

You can use a parsley mill (dry the herb thoroughly first, or it will go to a pulp) or a mezzalune, a specially curved knife blade that fits inside a wooden bowl. But there is probably no faster way than the one our grandmothers used, chopping herbs on a board with a knife.

1 Strip the leaves from the stalks unless, as with parsley, you wish to include some of the tender stalks for flavour.
2 Hold the tip of the knife on the board with the fingertips of your left hand. Pump the handle up and down with your right hand, chopping rhythmically and quickly. Swing the blade in an arc over the board to gather in stray leaves. Done in seconds!

GARLIC

This does so much to add flavour that crushing or chopping a garlic clove must become one of the reflex actions of cooking. Those who really profess to know maintain that there is only one way—pounding it with a little salt, using a pestle and mortar. I don't think it matters. Sometimes, though, the texture of crushed garlic is an obvious advantage—in a smooth pâté or dip, for example. I find the tong-like garlic presses quick and easy to use and am not aware of any loss of flavour.

It is easier to chop a peeled clove of garlic if you slightly crush it first. Put it on a board and hit it lightly from an inch or so above the board with the flat side of a cleaver or a rolling pin. Then chop it by holding the knife blade at both the point and the handle and making a series of rapid cuts first from left or right and then at right angles.

ONIONS

Chopping onions used to be the bane of my life. On fast-food days, I had only to see 'peel and chop one onion' in the recipe to be put off completely. But now I have learned to chop an onion the chef's way, with a very sharp knife. This is what you do.

1   Peel the onion and put it on a wooden board.
2   Cut it in half from stalk to root. Lay one half cut side down on the board.
3   Hold the onion firm with the fingers of your left hand, or use an onion holder—a tool like a short comb with long metal teeth.
4   Working from the stalk to the root end, make close vertical cuts which do not, however—and this is most important—cut completely through to the board.
5   Now, with your hand resting flat on top of the onion, make horizontal cuts parallel to the board, but still not cutting right through the onion to the end. All this while it will stay in one piece and not collapse on you.
6   Finally, slice it right through, making vertical cuts at right angles to the first ones. Now it should fall apart, in tiny neatly chopped pieces.

Slicing Meat

Meat is much easier to slice if it is almost frozen stiff—even chilling it for a few minutes makes all the difference. Put the unwrapped meat on a plate in the fast-freeze section of the freezer, or in the refrigerator.

To slice meat, put it on a wooden board and bang it once with a meat mallet, rolling pin or the side of a cleaver (see page 16). This not only helps to tenderize it, but makes it much easier to slice.

Slice all meat except poultry and veal escalopes across the grain, slantwise. To cut the very thin strips needed for beef stroganoff, for example, cut the whole piece of meat first into very thin diagonal slices. Without moving the meat, cut across the slices into strips the length you require.

It is essential to use a very good quality steel knife that is really sharp (see page 16).

TO USE A CLEAVER

1   Place the meat on a wooden board. Flatten it by striking once with the side of the cleaver.
2   Make a loose fist with your left hand and rest it on the meat. It is particularly important to get into the habit of holding the food in this way—it means that your fingers are tucked out of harm's way. Practise pushing the meat gradually to the right with your knuckles. The idea is that the cleaver falls on exactly the same spot each time; it is the food that is moved. As you push the food to the right, ease your knuckles back across it to the left.
3   Point the thumb and first finger of your right hand along the blade of the cleaver and clasp the handle, not too tightly, with the other three fingers. Hold the knife blade at right angles to the chopping board. Raise it no higher than the top of the knuckles of your left hand, then let it fall with a light but firm stroke, cutting through the food in a single action.

Breadcrumbs

You must use slightly stale bread for crumbs. This is always understood even when the recipe calls for 'fresh breadcrumbs'. What that really means is fresh-but-slightly-stale, as distinct from toasted or dried breadcrumbs. New bread gangs up into obstinately inseparable lumps.

Of course, you will use a blender to make breadcrumbs whenever possible. Otherwise rub the bread across the mesh of a wire sieve. This is far quicker and easier than using a grater, and kinder to the knuckles.

Fruit

APPLES AND PEARS

Before peeling cooking apples, dunk them for a few seconds in boiling water. The peel will then come away more readily. Use a stainless steel knife or parer; other blades are likely to leave a 'taste'.

Scoop out the core of ripe dessert pears with a teaspoon. It's just the right size and shape, and much quicker than using a knife.

LEMONS AND ORANGES

Whenever the lemon juice alone is needed, you can use Jif lemon juice, simple to squeeze from the plastic 'lemon' or to shake from the bottle. Store it in the refrigerator.

Before squeezing the juice from a lemon or orange, roll the fruit a few times on a board to make the juice run more easily.

And before peeling citrus fruit, drop them in boiling water for a few seconds to loosen the peel.

Use a potato peeler or a sharp stainless steel knife to pare thin strips of rind. To obtain just the zest, use a grater or a fruit zester (see page 18).

Marinating

When marinating meat or fish the quickest way is to put all the ingredients into a thick polythene bag, firmly seal the top with a twist tie and put it on a plate or in a dish in the refrigerator or a cool place. If you happen to be at home, occasionally turn the bag over. If the ingredient is something delicate, such as a whole fish, support the bag with your hand as you turn it, to avoid breaking the fish.

Measuring

When the accuracy of measurements is not vital to the last gram, using a teaspoon or tablespoon and shaking the ingredient to level it is quicker than a pair of weighing scales. That is why many 'spoon' measurements are given in the recipes throughout this book.

Drop by drop. To measure a few drops of food colouring or essence, dip a skewer into the bottle and shake off the drops. That way you will be sure of using only as little as you need.

A Fast Set-up

There's no point in getting the preparation and cooking of the meal down to a fine art, only to bump up against a time bomb when it comes to setting the table. No end of time can be wasted collecting all the various elements of table paraphernalia together: time that could be spent more profitably.

The first essential is to take stock of all the china and cutlery you are likely to need so that it is quick and easy to reach.

Front of the cupboard priority should always be given to the things that are used most. Pretty little knick-knacks and items that only come out for high days and Christmas holidays should be relegated to the back of the most inaccessible places—very high cupboards, or those at floor levels. The plates and dishes that will need warming before the meal might well be kept in the kitchen, close to the heat source, and sideboard space given only to the things that go straight on to the table. It might be worth considering keeping stacks of four or six plates at the ready on a trolley or side table in the dining-room. Only you will know whether you entertain people often enough to prevent them from getting dusty.

It goes without saying that glasses should be well polished before they are put away, so they are sparkling, twinkling clean the next time. Just to be sure, keep a clean towel beside them in the cupboard so that you can polish them in one movement as you put them on the table.

I find it easiest to store cutlery in place settings, each in its own polythene bag. If the bag is tied up at the top, clean silver will stay shining bright. Setting one place at a time round the table is quicker than setting six soup spoons, six dinner forks and so on.

The choice between a tablecloth and place mats is a personal one, and people tend to feel strongly one way or the other. If you are in the habit of inviting people to a meal every few days, and have a separate dining-room, you might get round the situation by putting a freshly-ironed cloth on the table and leaving it there ready and waiting. We can't do that, because the cats tend to think it's a new kind of bedspread! Table napkins that are put away neatly and crisply ironed, stay that way if you keep each set of six in a small flat box. Then they don't get curled up at the edges, like railway sandwiches, and don't need dashing over with a smoothing iron as the door bell rings. In case the napkins don't get ironed at all—or at least, not in time for the next occasion—I keep a stock of good-quality paper ones. Wipe heat-resisting table mats over with a damp cloth after each meal and keep them in the same drawer or cupboard as the cutlery and napkins, so that setting them is part of the same arm movement.

Put new candles in the candle holders, fill the salt and pepper pots, even the sugar bowl—all the things that could otherwise slow you down when your mind is on the food alone.

TABLE DECORATIONS

Faced with a dinner party and no flowers, how can you improvise a table decoration? For an informal meal in a farmhouse-type kitchen you can get by with a family group of those pretty little maize dolls, from America or Czechoslovakia, that carry bundles of firewood, flowers and washing. Arranged on a woven rush or cane place-mat they make quite a focal point. So, too do a group of glass-stoppered kitchen jars in different sizes. Pasta, dried fruits, dried peas and beans, all lovely to look at, would be a decidedly different still-life group, not a bit out of place in a homely setting. A basket of fir-cones, nuts or wrapped sweets scattered with a few sprays of leaves set the mood for a winter table, a bowl of apples or mixed fruit is as attractive as any flowers, and a pottery bowl of lemons, oranges or grapefruit at marmalade time is a real eyecatcher. One lovely table decoration I admired, the week before Easter, was a gypsy basket of deep speckled brown eggs and a few trails of ivy, with never a flower in sight.

3
ALWAYS IN STORE

I should have hated to live centuries ago, when provisions were laid down at the onset of winter and would not be replenished until the first harvest the following year. To see stocks of food gradually dwindling, and not be able to do anything about it—how utterly unnerving. And how limiting, in terms of menu planning.

Nowadays, with all the products of modern preservation methods at our disposal, we can stock our store-cupboards, refrigerators or freezers so that we always have on hand the main essentials for unplanned meals.

What exactly those items are will vary from one family to another. The amount of storage space you have; the distance you live from the shops, and what type of shops they are; how early and late they are open, and whether you are out of the home all day will have a bearing. And, whereas some of us take comfort from setting a little money aside each week to buy special offers in the supermarket or seasonal bargains on the market stalls, others like to live more dangerously.

As you read the recipes in this book, you will soon discover the main items you will need to make them. Most are the basic stand-bys that any busy cook hates to be without; others, such as herbs, seasonings and flavourings, tend to be matters of personal preference.

Refrigerator. Most of us use the refrigerator as a cold larder, and in many kitchens it is the only larder for fresh foods. (Check the instruction booklet for storage times in your freezing compartment; they vary considerably.) Food stored until it goes 'off' is at best a waste of money, at worst a health risk.

BASIC FOODS

	Storage times	
	Refrigerator	*Larder*
Butter, margarine, lard and cooking fats	3–4 weeks	1 week
Eggs	2 weeks	1 week
Milk	3–4 days	1 day
Cheese, hard	2–3 weeks	1 week
soft	1 week	1–2 days

OPTIONAL EXTRAS

	Storage times	
	Refrigerator	*Larder*
Yoghurt and fresh soured cream	1 week	1–2 days
Double and single cream	3–4 days	1 day
Mayonnaise (home-made, see pp. 173, 175)	1 week	2 days
Bacon	1 week	2–3 days
Salami and other smoked meats	3 months	1 month
Hard-boiled eggs	1 week	1–2 days
Salad vegetables	4–5 days	2–3 days
Green or red pepper	2 weeks	5–7 days

DRIED AND CANNED GOODS

Apart from the basics such as flour, cornflour, long- and short-grain rice, breakfast cereals (for toppings and garnishes) and sugar, try to keep a good selection of pasta. Plain and green noodles, 'instant' lasagne that does not need pre-cooking, spaghetti, macaroni and pasta shapes such as shells and wagon wheels are not only the foundation of many a fast meal, they also take the place of potatoes and other vegetables when you need an instant accompaniment to the main dish. Pasta can be stored in a dry, cool place for 10–12 months.

Chicken and beef stock cubes, packets of sauce mix, whole and ground spices, dried herbs, flavoured vinegars, bottled sauces such as soy, hot red pepper, Worcestershire and tomato ketchup all help to give your basic ingredients on-the-spot personality.

Canned fish is invaluable for first courses, quick sauces to serve with pasta and rice, and savouries-on-toast for quick snacks or to finish a meal. Sardines, anchovies, prawns and tuna are particularly versatile.

Among the canned soups, condensed consommé (stored in the refrigerator) inspires the most imaginative efforts—being double-strength, it is set to a thicker jelly consistency and cuts up well to fill avocados or mix with salads, for example. Ordinary-strength consommé and canned lobster and crab bisques can be made extra special with no more than a dash of sherry.

Canned fruit, fruit juices, and vegetables can be life-savers; black cherries, figs, lychees, orange and tomato juice, asparagus spears, kidney beans, salsify, we all have our special favourites.

Find room for a can of freeze-dried milk for the non-milkman days, cans of cream to enrich soups and sauces, and perhaps cans of ham and a couple of good, smooth pâtés. Instant pudding mixes, even if you do not like them on their own, can be dressed up into some quite delicious concoctions, and make good flan fillings and toppings. A selection of biscuits, savoury to serve with soups, pâté and cheese, and sweet and semi-sweet to offer with creamy puddings, is a must.

If your cooking for a crowd is erratic you will not want to run the risk of buying fresh vegetables regularly, but there is always a case for having a few onions on hand. They keep well and are particularly indispensable. A bowl of fresh fruit, even if it consists of no more than a couple of bags of well-polished apples, is as good an 'after' as any; include a lemon and orange and you always have them ready for pre-dinner drinks.

4
FIRST COURSES
All recipes serve 6

When every second counts, it can be tempting to skip the first course and go straight into the main dish. Don't. You actually lose time by doing this. All the while people are enjoying the opening course, however simple it is, every minute is precious to you. The meat for the next course can be continuing along its way to succulent tenderness, the vegetables braising to perfection and the rice drying off.

It is up to the cook to determine how long people will take to enjoy this course. You can plan to gain time by choosing a starter that they will linger over, such as a light, creamy mousse or pâté eaten with 'dip-sticks' of raw crispy vegetables. I defy anyone to crunch their way through all that natural fibre before I am ready for them. And if things are a little slow in the kitchen, you can toss in an absolutely fascinating piece of gossip or a remark that warrants quite a bit of discussion, and add valuable minutes to the cooking schedule. Being a good host or hostess doesn't just mean being a good cook!

Do everything you possibly can to cut down on the last-minute preparations. All the recipes in the Starting from Scratch sections can have minutes clipped off them if you can do one or two things before you go to bed or dash out to the office. If you will be using goods from store, try to put them out ready to use as soon as you get in. Scrabble among your canned goods and get out the tuna fish, prawns or kidney beans you will need, fight your way to the back of the cupboard for bottles of sauce or mustard you don't often use, and put the lemon, onion, carrots or green pepper ready on the chopping board with the appropriate knives. Put canned consommé in the refrigerator if it needs to be chilled. Take the frozen prawns or green beans from the freezing compartment and put them on a plate in the refrigerator to thaw during the day, then you won't have to dunk them frantically in hot water at the last minute.

Get out the electric toaster and leave it ready to plug in. Or plan to pass a shop during the day where you can buy some really super bread, French sticks, granary or wholemeal, pitta or rye, whatever goes best with the dish.

If you have time, make the French dressing and leave it in a lidded jar. Make the garlic butter and leave it foil-wrapped in the refrigerator. Chop the parsley and mushrooms and leave them in a covered container. Chop the walnuts and hard-boil the eggs. Get out the mixing bowls and pans you will need. Any one of these jobs done in advance will give you not only more time but more confidence as you start preparing the meal.

Starting from Scratch

Melon Salad

A sweet and sour, smooth and crunchy salad of contrasts.

small honeydew or Lavan melon	3 tbsp natural yoghurt
50 g (2 oz) chopped walnuts	2 tbsp chopped parsley
50 g (2 oz) seedless raisins	small onion
75 ml (⅛ pt) French dressing	Chinese leaves to serve (optional)

1 Halve the melon, cut the flesh away from the skin and discard the seeds. Dice the flesh and put it into a bowl.
2 Add the chopped walnuts and the raisins and stir in the French dressing and yoghurt. Reserving a little chopped parsley to garnish, stir in the rest.
3 Peel the onion and cut into thin rings. Carefully stir these into the salad.
4 Serve the salad on Chinese leaves, if available, or piled into a glass bowl. Sprinkle with chopped parsley to garnish and serve well chilled.

Watermelon Creole

½ sugar baby watermelon	1 tbsp chopped parsley
300 ml (½ pt) mayonnaise	198-g (7-oz) can tuna fish
2 tsp curry powder	parsley sprigs to garnish
2 tsp tomato purée	

1 Scoop out the melon flesh into balls, using a melon baller or a teaspoon. Reserve a few of the best shapes to garnish, and put the rest in a bowl.
2 Mix together the mayonnaise, curry powder, tomato purée and chopped parsley and, using a wooden spoon, combine them with the melon.

3   Drain the tuna fish, flake it and stir it into the mayonnaise.
4   Divide the salad between 6 tall glasses or small fruit dishes, and garnish each with the reserved melon balls and the parsley sprigs. Serve well chilled.

Grapefruit and Avocado Salad

Canned grapefruit, with its rough texture and sharp flavour, benefits from the smooth blandness of avocado.

3 medium-sized avocados
539-g (1 lb 3-oz) can grapefruit
   segments
150 ml ($\frac{1}{4}$pt) French dressing

1 large head chicory
1 large lemon
cayenne pepper to garnish

1   Peel the avocados, halve them and remove the stones. Cut the flesh in slices.
2   Drain the grapefruit segments.
3   Pour the French dressing into a shallow dish and, using wooden spoons, gently turn the grapefruit segments and avocado slices in it.
4   Trim, wash and dry the chicory leaves. Divide them between 6 small plates and arrange alternate slices of avocado and grapefruit on them.
5   Cut the lemon into 6 wedges and put one on to each plate.
6   Just before serving, pour any remaining French dressing over each salad and sprinkle a pinch of cayenne pepper over the fruit.

Avocado Waldorf Salad

3 tender stalks celery, cleaned
2 crisp eating apples
3 medium-sized avocados
150 ml ($\frac{1}{4}$pt) single cream

a pinch of grated nutmeg
a pinch of ground cloves
40 g (1$\frac{1}{2}$oz) walnuts, chopped

1   Cut the celery into thin strips.
2   Core the apples and chop the flesh into slightly smaller cubes.
3   Peel the avocados, halve them, remove the stones and chop the flesh into cubes.
4   Using a wooden spoon, mix these ingredients together and stir in the single cream. Season lightly with nutmeg and cloves.
5   Serve in individual dishes or ramekins, garnished with the chopped walnuts.

Avocado with Jellied Soup

This dish is instant as long as you have two cans of condensed consommé in the refrigerator.

2 298-g (10½-oz) cans condensed
  consommé, chilled
3 medium-sized avocados

a few watercress sprigs
2 lemons

1 Tip the solidified condensed soup on to a chopping board and cut into 1-cm (½-in) cubes.
2 Halve the avocados, remove the stones and set the fruit in serving dishes or on small plates.
3 Pile the jellied cubes into the avocado halves and garnish with watercress sprigs.
4 Serve well chilled, with lemon wedges.

Avocado with Tuna Sauce

150-ml (5 fl-oz) carton soured
  cream
4 tsp Worcestershire sauce
1 heaped tsp tomato purée
small onion or 2 spring onions
salt

freshly ground black pepper
1 tbsp lemon juice
198-g (7-oz) can tuna fish
3 avocados
1 large lemon
parsley sprigs to garnish

1 Beat together the soured cream, Worcestershire sauce and tomato purée.
2 Peel the onion or trim the spring onions, chop finely and add to the sauce. Season with salt and pepper and add to the lemon juice.
3 Thoroughly drain the tuna fish and flake it into the bowl.
4 Halve the avocados and remove the stones. Set them into dishes or on to small plates and divide the sauce between them.
5 Cut the lemon into 6 wedges. Garnish the avocados with a lemon wedge and parsley sprigs.

Shrimp Avocado

3 medium-sized avocados
2 small cartons potted shrimps

a pinch of cayenne pepper
2 small lemons

1 Halve the avocados and remove the stones. Put the halves in serving dishes or on to small plates.
2 Tip the potted shrimps into a bowl, break up the solidified

butter with a fork, and season the shrimps with a pinch of
cayenne pepper.
3   Strain the juice of ½ a lemon (reserve the rest for garnish) and
mix it into the shrimps.
4   Divide the shrimp mixture between the 6 avocado halves.
5   Cut the remaining lemons into quarters and use for garnish.
Serve cayenne pepper on the table. Wholemeal or rye bread is a
good accompaniment.

Tuna and Avocado Salad (See Plate 4)

Quick to assemble and an attractive centrepiece to start the meal,
this salad uses 'refrigerator vegetables' and a can of tuna fish.

1 Cos lettuce, or Chinese leaves   *15 ml (1 tbsp) lemon juice*
4 large, firm tomatoes   *198-g (7-oz) can tuna fish*
2 avocados   *garlic salad dressing (page 178)*

1   Wash and dry the salad leaves and line a salad bowl with them.
2   Thickly slice the tomatoes into a mixing bowl.
3   Peel the avocados, halve them and remove the stones. Thinly
slice the flesh and toss it in the lemon juice. Add the slices to the
tomatoes in the bowl.
4   Roughly flake the tuna fish into the bowl. Pour on the garlic
dressing and gently toss the ingredients together. Spoon the
tuna salad on to the lettuce leaves just before serving.

Avocado Cream

This smooth, slightly tangy cream is very rich; serve in small
individual dishes.

3 medium-sized avocados   *salt*
150 ml (¼ pt) single cream   *freshly ground black pepper*
1 tsp tomato ketchup   *12 walnut halves*
thin Yorkshire Relish

1   Peel the avocados, halve them, remove the stones and roughly
chop the flesh.
2   Put the avocado in a blender with the cream, tomato ketchup
and a few drops of Yorkshire Relish, and season with a little salt
and pepper.
3   Blend until the mixture is smooth. Taste it and add more sauce
and seasoning if required. The mixture should have a slight

'bite' to it. If you do not have a blender, mash the avocado in a bowl with a fork.

4   Pour the cream into 6 serving dishes and cover them with cling film. Leave them in the refrigerator until you are ready to serve.
5   Garnish each dish with 2 walnut halves. It is good served with hot toast or crispbread biscuits.

Anchovy Cheese

This is a cheese dip strongly flavoured with anchovies—a little goes a long way.

50-g (1¾-oz) can anchovy fillets
275 g (10 oz) cream cheese
3 tbsp double cream
2 tsp chopped parsley
1 tsp anchovy essence
a pinch of cayenne pepper

parsley sprigs to garnish
selection of crudités—carrot or cucumber sticks, cauliflower florets, green pepper strips, mushroom halves, salted crackers, Twiglets

1   Drain the anchovy fillets. Remove any bones and pat the fillets dry with kitchen paper. Chop or cut them finely.
2   Mix together the cream cheese, cream, parsley and anchovy essence, or blend the ingredients in a blender. Add the chopped anchovies and season with a pinch of cayenne pepper. If the mixture is too stiff, moisten it with a little more cream.
3   Divide the cheese mixture between 6 individual ramekin dishes and garnish each one with a parsley sprig.
4   Prepare the crudités according to type. Peel or scrape the carrots, trim them and push them through a potato chipper, or cut them into strips. Divide the cauliflower into florets—reserve the stalk and leaves to make soup. Trim the green pepper and cut it into strips.
5   Put each ramekin dish on a small plate and surround it by your chosen crudités, arranged in groups for the best colour contrast.

Smoked Salmon Mousse

Most delicatessens sell smoked salmon 'off-cuts' considerably cheaper than the regular price; they are ideal for this mousse.

175 g (6 oz) smoked salmon off-cuts
350 g (12 oz) full-fat cream cheese
2 tbsp yoghurt, chilled

freshly ground black pepper
cayenne pepper
1 red pepper (optional)

1   Roughly cut up the smoked salmon and put it into the blender bowl with the cream cheese and yoghurt. Whizz for a few seconds to make a smooth, creamy paste, and season to taste.
2   If you are using frozen smoked salmon which has lost some of its subtle flavour, trim a red pepper, roughly chop it and blend it with the salmon and cheese mixture. It does wonders.
3   Divide the mousse between 6 little dishes and garnish each with a little sprinkled cayenne pepper. Good with hot toast or wholemeal crispbreads.

Prawns in Spiced Mayonnaise

Horseradish gives that little 'something' that frozen prawns often need—piquancy.

1 large red pepper, or 1 canned
  pimento
1 large clove garlic
450 g (1 lb) prawns, thawed
450 ml (¾ pt) mayonnaise

3 tbsp creamed horseradish
freshly ground black pepper
cayenne pepper
1 large lemon

1   Trim the red pepper, discarding the seeds, and finely chop it, or chop the canned pimento.
2   Peel and crush the garlic.
3   Mix all the ingredients together, reserving a few prawns to garnish. Season well with black pepper and to taste with cayenne pepper.
4   Pile the mixture into a serving dish, or into individual dishes. Garnish with the reserved prawns lightly sprinkled with cayenne pepper, and serve with a wedge of lemon.

Bean and Bean Sprout Salad

425-g (15-oz) can red kidney beans
225 g (8 oz) bean sprouts, fresh if
  possible

1 small onion
1 dsp chopped parsley
250 ml (scant ½ pt) French dressing

1   Drain the canned beans.
2   Wash and drain the bean sprouts.
3   Peel and thinly slice the onion.
4   Mix all the ingredients together, reserving a little parsley to sprinkle over as a garnish.

Bean and Mushroom Salad

450 g (1 lb) green beans, thawed
450 g (1 lb) button mushrooms
1 small onion
1 small clove garlic
1 tbsp chopped parsley

300 ml (½ pt) French dressing
2 medium-sized tomatoes
salt
freshly ground black pepper

1 Leave the beans in a colander to thaw.
2 Wipe, trim and slice the mushrooms. Peel and thinly slice the onion. Peel and crush the garlic.
3 Mix together the onion, garlic, parsley and French dressing and toss in the thawed beans and the mushrooms.
4 Arrange on a flat dish, garnished with sliced tomatoes. Season the tomatoes with a little salt and grind black pepper generously over the salad.

Celeriac in Mustard Mayonnaise

You must slice the vegetables really thinly.

1 large root celeriac
2 large carrots
250 ml (scant ½ pt) mayonnaise

1 tbsp Meaux mustard
freshly ground black pepper

1 Trim and wash the celeriac, discarding any discoloured parts. Using a very sharp kitchen knife, cut it into matchstick strips.
2 Scrape and trim the carrots. Grate about 2 teaspoons and set aside to garnish. Cut the remainder into matchstick strips.
3 Mix the mustard into the mayonnaise and stir in the Julienne strips of vegetables.
4 Pile on to a serving dish, grind some black pepper over, and garnish with the grated carrot.

Frankfurter and Fennel Salad

1 root of fennel
1 small onion
6 small frankfurter sausages
  (canned ones are fine)

150 ml (¼ pt) French dressing
1 tsp Dijon mustard
½ tsp mixed dried herbs

1 Trim and wash the fennel, discarding any discoloured parts. Slice it thinly.

2 Peel and thinly slice the onion.
3 Trim the frankfurter sausages and slice them slantwise.
4 Put the French dressing in a bowl, stir in the mustard and herbs and toss in the vegetables and sausage.
5 Turn into a shallow serving dish. Especially good with pumpernickel or rye bread.

Yoghurt and Cucumber Soup

This old Turkish recipe is ideal to serve in the garden, or before a spicy main dish.

1 medium-sized cucumber
2 large cloves garlic
1 tbsp fresh mint leaves
450 ml (¾pt) chilled yoghurt
salt
freshly ground black pepper
a few sprigs fresh mint leaves

1 Peel the cucumber, cut it in half lengthways, and scoop out and discard the seeds. Grate the cucumber flesh into a bowl.
2 Peel and crush the garlic cloves and add them to the cucumber.
3 Chop and mix in the mint leaves, add the yoghurt and season well with salt and pepper.
4 Cover the bowl and keep it in the refrigerator.
5 Serve the soup in chilled bowls garnished with the mint sprigs.

Prawn and Cucumber Soup

Chill the soup bowls before serving.

600 ml (1 pt) chilled yoghurt
300 ml (½pt) single cream
1 medium-sized cucumber
1 heaped tbsp mint leaves
175 g (6 oz) prawns, thawed
salt
freshly ground black pepper
cayenne pepper to garnish
sprigs of mint to garnish

1 Mix together the yoghurt and cream.
2 Peel the cucumber, scrape out the seeds and grate or liquidize the flesh.
3 Chop the mint leaves.
4 Mix the cucumber, prawns and mint into the yoghurt mixture, taste and season with a little salt and plenty of pepper.
5 Serve in the chilled bowls garnished with a pinch of cayenne pepper and sprigs of mint.

Asparagus and Mushroom Soup

The addition of mushrooms offsets the slightly 'tart' flavour that canned asparagus has.

50 g (2 oz) butter
1 medium-sized onion
175 g (6 oz) mushrooms
50 g (2 oz) flour
900 ml (1½ pts) milk, hot
1 bay leaf

400-g (15-oz) can asparagus
  spears
2 tbsp dry sherry
salt
freshly ground black pepper
cream, single or soured, to garnish

1 Melt the butter in a pan.
2 Peel and slice the onion. Trim and halve the mushrooms. Cook them over a moderate heat for 3–4 minutes.
3 Stir in the flour and gradually add the milk and asparagus liquor, stirring until it boils. Add the bay leaf.
4 Reserving a few strips to garnish, chop the asparagus and add it to the soup. Add the sherry and season well with salt and pepper. Simmer for 10 minutes. Remove the bay leaf.
5 Swirl a little cream or fresh soured cream on top and garnish with the reserved asparagus tips.

Shellfish Consommé

Nothing to cook—just a quick assembly job.

2 298-g (10½-oz) cans condensed
  consommé, chilled
175 g (6 oz) frozen prawns, thawed
2 tbsp medium sherry

a pinch of cayenne pepper
freshly ground black pepper
2 small peppers, 1 green, 1 red
1 large lemon

1 Tip out the chilled consommé, cut it into cubes and divide it between 6 chilled individual soup dishes.
2 Toss the prawns in the sherry and season them well with pepper and a pinch of cayenne pepper.
3 Trim the green and red peppers and chop them finely.
4 Divide the prawns and peppers between the dishes.
5 Cut the lemon into 6 wedges and garnish each dish. Serve well chilled.

Melt-in-the-Mouth Cheese

If you have a fondue burner or a plate warmer with nightlights, here is a simple first course that gets the meal off to a good start while people help themselves and pass the dish round and round.

150 ml (¼ pt) dry white wine
1 tsp lemon juice
375 g (14 oz) Gouda cheese
1 tbsp cornflour

1 tsp prepared English mustard
freshly ground black pepper
1 French loaf to serve

1   Heat the wine (reserving 1 dessertspoonful) and lemon juice in a heavy pan until nearly boiling.
2   Grate the cheese and gradually add to the liquid, beating with a wooden spoon.
3   Blend the cornflour with the reserved wine until it forms a smooth, thin paste. Add it to the cheese mixture, beating well. Beat in the mustard and season well with pepper.
4   Transfer the fondue to heated fondue dish or flameproof casserole and set it over a burner.
5   Cut the French loaf into bite-sized pieces and pile them up on a dish or basket. Provide a fork for each person to spear the bread and dip it into the hot fondue.

Mushrooms in Garlic Butter

Make sure that everyone enjoys garlic, for without it you destroy the essence of the dish.

450 g (1 lb) mushrooms
75 g (3 oz) butter (or ready-made garlic butter, page 171)
2 large cloves garlic (omit if using garlic butter)

1 heaped tbsp chopped parsley
salt
freshly ground black pepper
1 lemon

1   Wipe, trim and slice the mushrooms thickly, leaving the stalks on.
2   Heat the butter in a frying-pan.
3   Peel and crush the garlic. Sauté the garlic and mushrooms over a moderate heat for 4–5 minutes, when the mushrooms should be just tender.
4   Toss in the parsley, season with salt and pepper and turn into a heated serving dish. Serve very hot, with a wedge of lemon and French bread.

Mushrooms in Soured Cream

Based on a Hungarian dish, this blend of black and white, mushrooms and soured cream, is lightly spiced with paprika.

50 g (2 oz) butter
1 small onion
1 tsp paprika
325 g (12 oz) mushrooms

salt
150 ml (5 fl oz) soured cream
parsley sprigs to garnish

1   Heat the butter in a frying-pan.
2   Peel and finely slice the onion and sauté it over a moderate heat for 3 minutes. Sprinkle on the paprika, stir well and add the mushrooms. Season with salt and braise for about 6 minutes until the mushrooms are tender and the liquid is reduced. Pour on the soured cream and allow to heat through.
3   Turn into a heated serving dish and garnish with parsley sprigs. It is good with hot pitta bread, or warm wholemeal rolls.

Prawns in Garlic Butter

This gives the impression that a lot of care and attention has been lavished on it. Illusion!

75 g (3 oz) butter (or ready-made
*   garlic butter, page 171)*
2 large cloves garlic (omit if using
*   garlic butter)*
1 small onion

325 g (12 oz) prawns, thawed
1 tbsp chopped parsley
salt and cayenne pepper
freshly ground black pepper
1 lemon

1   Melt the butter in a frying-pan.
2   Peel and thinly slice the onion. Peel and crush the garlic. Sauté them in the butter, over a moderate heat, for about 4 minutes.
3   Add the prawns, shake the pan to coat them well with butter and cook for a further 4 minutes, during which time they should thoroughly absorb the flavour.
4   Stir in the parsley, season with a little·salt and with black and cayenne pepper to taste. Turn on to a heated serving dish, and serve piping hot with a wedge of lemon and, ideally, French bread.

Prawns in Cream Sauce

A delicious way to pamper your guests.

25 g (1 oz) butter
325 g (12 oz) prawns, thawed
2 tbsp dry white wine
150 ml (¼pt) double cream

2 tbsp soured cream
salt
freshly ground black pepper
paprika pepper to garnish

1   Heat the butter in a frying-pan.
2   Add the prawns and sauté them for about 3 minutes, shaking the pan at least once.
3   Pour in the wine and bring to the boil.
4   Add the cream and soured cream and heat gently. Taste and season with a little salt, and black pepper. Turn into a heated serving dish and garnish with a sprinkling of paprika. Warm wholemeal bread rolls are good with this.

Pasta with Tuna Sauce

Double the quantities to make a substantial main dish.

450 g (1 lb) fresh green noodles (fettucine), or 325 g (12 oz) dried pasta
25 g (1 oz) butter
2 tbsp olive oil
1 small onion

198-g (7-oz) can tuna fish
250 ml (scant ½ pt) chicken stock, or use stock cube
freshly ground black pepper
1 heaped tsp dried oregano
Parmesan cheese to serve

1   Cook the pasta in plenty of boiling, salted water until just tender—5–6 minutes for fresh pasta, or according to the directions on the packet. Drain in a colander, refresh with cold water and drain again. Melt the butter in the pan and shake the pasta in it, over a low heat.
2   Meanwhile heat the olive oil in a pan.
3   Peel and chop the onion and cook in the pan for 2–3 minutes over a moderate heat.
4   Drain and flake the tuna fish and add it to the onion in the pan. Stir with a wooden spoon, then add the stock, season well with pepper and add the herb. Cover and simmer for 5 minutes.
5   Tip the pasta into a greased and heated serving dish and pour the sauce over it. Serve with grated Parmesan cheese.

Pasta with Cheese and Cream

Plenty of cheese, and melting cream, make a simple and delicious sauce. Double the quantity for a main course.

450 g (1 lb) fresh green noodles (fettucine) or 325 g (12 oz) dried pasta
15 g (½ oz) butter

175 g (6 oz) Parmesan cheese
150 ml (¼ pt) double cream
freshly ground black pepper

1 Cook the pasta as described in the previous recipe.
2 Put the butter in a deep serving dish and heat it. Turn the drained pasta into the heated dish and stir in the grated cheese and the cream. Serve at once, generously sprinkled with black pepper.

With a Little Forethought

If you can give a little time to the first course the evening or morning before the meal, then your repertoire can include simple creams, mousses and pâtés that need time to set and chill, and soups that take a while to reach a flavour blend.

Club Melon

After several hours the wine is absorbed into the fruit, imparting a rich flavour and a deep colour.

1 large melon
1 generous wine glass port or
 sweet sherry

6 maraschino cherries
1 large lemon

1   Slice the top from the melon and, using a tablespoon, scoop out and discard all the loose membrane and the seeds. Stand the melon upright in a bowl.
2   Pour in the port or sherry, tipping the melon slightly so that the wine swishes all round inside it. Replace the melon lid, wrap the fruit in foil and put it in the refrigerator to chill overnight or throughout the day.
3   To serve the melon, cut it into 6 wedges. If you have time, cut the melon flesh away from the skin and chop it, still resting on the skin, into cubes.
4   Put wedges of lemon and the cherries on to 6 cocktail sticks and spear them into the melon wedges.

You can vary this dish—more cheaply—by substituting ginger wine for the port or sherry. In this case, omit the cherry garnish. You can replace it with a slice of preserved ginger.

Mushroom Salad

The flavour and texture of the mushrooms are best if they can be left to marinate in the dressing for an hour or two.

225 g (8 oz) button mushrooms   salt
1 small onion   freshly ground black pepper
1 large clove garlic   1 heaped tbsp chopped parsley
250 ml (scant ½ pt) French dressing

1   Wipe and trim the mushrooms and, leaving the stalks on, slice
    them thinly.
2   Peel and thinly slice the onion. Peel and crush the garlic.
3   Stir the onion and garlic into the French dressing and toss in the
    mushrooms. Season with salt and pepper. If leaving to mari-
    nate, cover and chill in the refrigerator.
4   Before serving, stir in most of the parsley, reserving a little to
    garnish. Turn into a bowl and sprinkle the rest of the parsley on
    top.

Cheese Castles

Dariole moulds or yoghurt pots, straight sided and easy to turn
out, give good effect to a simple cheese and vegetable salad.

325 g (12 oz) Gouda cheese   pinch of cayenne pepper
75 g (3 oz) cooked long-grain rice   freshly ground black pepper
1 red pepper   4 medium-sized tomatoes
1 head celery, washed

1   Grate the cheese into a bowl and mix it with the rice.
2   Trim the red pepper, removing seeds, and chop it finely.
3   Finely chop 2 stalks of the celery and add it, with the red
    pepper, to the cheese mixture. Season with pepper.
4   Cut the tomatoes into slices. Put a slice in the base of each of 6
    moulds.
5   Spoon some of the cheese mixture into each mould. Add
    another tomato slice, more cheese, pressing it well down, and
    finish with a tomato slice. Leave in the refrigerator to become
    firm while you prepare the main course.
6   Run a knife round the moulds and turn them out on to a plate.
    Grate more black pepper over the top and serve with celery
    sticks.

Liver and Olive Pâté

Here is a pâté that is very quick to make so it can be done a little in
advance: the butter coating keeps it from drying out.

175 g (6 oz) butter   2 tbsp brandy
1 medium-sized onion   salt
1 large clove garlic   freshly ground black pepper
325 g (12 oz) chicken livers   12 Spanish stuffed green olives
1 tsp mixed dried herbs

1   Melt 50 g (2 oz) of the butter in a frying-pan.
2   Peel and chop the onion. Peel and crush the garlic.
3   Cook the onion, garlic and livers in the butter for 5–6 minutes
    over a moderate heat.
4   Add the herbs and cook for a further 2–3 minutes, breaking up
    the livers with a wooden spoon.
5   Put the mixture into a blender with the brandy and a further
    50 g (2 oz) melted butter, and add the seasoning. Blend to a
    smooth paste. If you do not have a blender, chop the mixture
    finely with a fork and beat it well with a wooden spoon until it is
    smooth.
6   Pour the pâté into 6 individual ramekin dishes and smooth the
    tops with a knife. Melt the remaining butter and pour it over the
    pâté. Leave the dishes in the refrigerator to set.
7   Decorate each dish with sliced olives. Serve chilled with hot
    toast or—just as good—Dutch crispbake rounds.

Liver and Mushroom Pâté

Very quick to make, but it needs to be made an hour or so in
advance.

50 g (2 oz) butter   ½ tsp mixed dried herbs
1 medium-sized onion   salt
1 large clove garlic   freshly ground black pepper
225 g (8 oz) chicken livers   whole black olives and sprigs of
215-g (7½-oz) can creamed   watercress to garnish
    mushrooms

1   Melt the butter in a frying-pan.
2   Peel and chop the onion. Peel and crush the garlic.
3   Cook the onion, garlic and livers in the pan for 5–6 minutes,
    breaking up the livers with a wooden spoon as they become
    pale and crumbly.
4   Transfer the cooked mixture to a blender and blend for a few
    seconds to make a smooth paste.
5   Turn the mixture into a bowl and beat in the mushrooms, herbs
    and seasoning.

6   Pour the pâté into a pottery dish, cover and leave in the refrigerator to chill.
7   Decorate the top of the pâté with glistening black olive flowers and sprays of watercress 'leaves'. Serve with hot toast or Dutch crispbake rounds.

Mackerel Pâté

The ingredients can be quickly blended together the night or morning before and left to set.

4 smoked mackerel fillets
1 lemon, juice and grated rind
100 g (4 oz) cream cheese
225 g (8 oz) butter, melted
salt

freshly ground black pepper

For the topping
50 g (2 oz) butter, melted
25 g (1 oz) stuffed green olives

1   Skin and flake the mackerel fillets.
2   Put half the mackerel fillets in the blender with half the remaining ingredients. Blend until the pâté is smooth. Repeat with the second batch.
3   Pour the mixture into a pottery terrine or small casserole and smooth the top.
4   Pour on the melted butter, tipping the dish so that the butter reaches the sides. Cover the dish and leave it in the refrigerator for the butter to set.
5   Slice the olives and decorate the top of the pâté. Serve with fingers of hot toast or Dutch Crispbake rounds.

Egg and Shrimp Cocktail

No need for fiddly preparation of lettuce. Simply serve this fish cocktail in individual dishes or on hollowed-out cucumber.

4 hard-boiled eggs
175 g (6 oz) shelled shrimps
150 ml ($\frac{1}{4}$ pt) mayonnaise
150 ml ($\frac{1}{4}$ pt) red wine

150 ml (5 fl oz) soured cream
salt and cayenne pepper
1 cucumber (optional)

1   Cool, shell and chop the hard-boiled eggs.
2   Put the chopped eggs in a bowl and mix in the remaining main ingredients. Taste and season with salt and cayenne. Chill.
3   If you have time, trim a cucumber and cut it into three; cut each piece in half lengthways. Scoop out the seeds, using a melon baller or teaspoon. Put the cucumber 'boats' on separate plates

and spoon the shrimp mixture on top. Sprinkle a little cayenne pepper to garnish. Or spoon the cocktail into individual dishes or glasses. Lightly sprinkle with cayenne pepper.

Gazpacho

As the soup is to be blended, the vegetables need be only roughly cut or chopped for quickness and this can be done in advance.

795-g (1 lb 12-oz) can tomatoes
1 small onion
1 small green pepper
½ cucumber
1 large clove garlic
150 ml (¼pt) olive oil
4 tbsp white wine vinegar
150 ml (¼pt) chicken stock, or use
    stock cube

salt
freshly ground black pepper

For the garnish
hot red pepper sauce
1 tbsp chopped parsley; 12 Spanish
    stuffed green olives; croûtons; 2
    small onions, peeled and sliced
    into rings

1   Empty half the can of tomatoes into the blender bowl, ready to blend the soup in 2 batches.
2   Peel and roughly chop the onion. Trim and cut up the green pepper. Peel and roughly chop the cucumber. Peel and crush the garlic.
3   Add half the prepared vegetables to the tomatoes in the blender together with half the oil, vinegar and stock. Blend until the soup is smooth. Pour into a bowl.
4   Blend the second batch of soup. Taste and season well with salt, pepper and a few drops of hot pepper sauce. Chill the soup in a covered container.
5   Sprinkle the soup with the chopped parsley, and serve sliced olives, onion rings and croûtons separately for guests to help themselves.

Floating Gazpacho

Chopped vegetables are suspended in a near-jelly-like stock. You can prepare them well in advance.

795-g (1 lb 12-oz) can peeled
    tomatoes
900 ml (1½pts) chicken stock, or
    use stock cube
100 g (4 oz) fresh breadcrumbs
2 tbsp olive oil
2 tbsp red wine vinegar
6 tbsp dry white wine

2 medium-sized green peppers
1 large onion
2 large cloves garlic
½ small cucumber
salt
freshly ground black pepper
2 tbsp chopped parsley
croûtons to garnish (optional)

1 Empty the can of tomatoes into a blender and whizz for a few seconds until blended.
2 Tip into a large covered plastic bowl and stir in the stock, breadcrumbs, olive oil, wine vinegar and wine.
3 Trim and finely chop the peppers. Peel and chop the onion. Peel and crush the garlic. Cut the cucumber into quarters lengthways, then chop small—a quick way to deal with it, giving you quarter-circles.
4 Stir the vegetables into the soup, season well, and add most of the chopped parsley, reserving a little to garnish. Cover the bowl and chill overnight or all day in the refrigerator.
5 Serve garnished with the reserved parsley, if possible with croûtons.

Plum Soup

Canned fruit can produce some delightful surprises—such as this zingy cold soup.

3 450-g (1-lb) cans red plums
300 ml (½ pt) reserved syrup
300 ml (½ pt) red wine
½ tsp ground mixed spice
a pinch of ground cloves

2 tbsp lemon juice
1 tbsp cornflour
300 ml (½ pt) buttermilk
soured cream and nutmeg to
   garnish

1 Strain the plums and reserve the syrup. Press the plums through a sieve—the sieving attachment to an electric mixer does the job in seconds, but it doesn't take long anyway.
2 Put the plum purée, measured syrup, wine, spices and lemon juice in a saucepan and bring to the boil.
3 Stir the cornflour into a little water to make a smooth paste and add it to the plum mixture. Stir all the time until the mixture comes back to the boil, becomes clear and thickens. Taste and add a little sugar if you like, though the soup should not taste sweet. Allow to cool, then chill.
4 Stir in the buttermilk. Serve the soup in a chilled bowl with swirls of soured cream sprinkled with grated nutmeg.

Mainly from Store

Baked Grapefruit

Canned grapefruit segments are delicious baked with rum or brandy butter.

2 539-g (1 lb 3-oz) cans grapefruit
   segments
225 g (8 oz) rum butter (page 172)
grated nutmeg

2 tbsp rum to serve
25 g (1 oz) toasted almonds (page
   183)

1   Thoroughly drain the grapefruit segments into a colander, and toss them dry on kitchen paper.
2   Put the grapefruit into a shallow ovenproof dish. Cut the rum butter and scatter it over them, sprinkle lightly with grated nutmeg and cover the dish with foil. Bake at 190 °C (375 °F), Gas 5, for 15 minutes, until the rum butter is melted and gooey.
3   Sprinkle with the rum and toasted almonds.

If you do not have any rum or brandy butter, scatter 100 g (4 oz) dark brown sugar over the drained grapefruit, cut 100 g (4 oz) butter over it and pour on 2 tablespoons rum, brandy, Marsala, sweet sherry or Madeira. As the alcohol is driven off in the cooking, pour over a little more of the spirit or wine as you serve the dish.

Tuna Consommé

Take three tins from the store-cupboard and you have a soup in the time it takes to heat it.

2 298-g (10½-oz) cans condensed
   consommé
1 lemon
freshly ground black pepper
198-g (7-oz) can tuna fish

4 tbsp medium sherry
croûtons to garnish (optional)
1 tsp chopped parsley
Twiglets or Gristicks to serve

1   Put the consommé in a pan with the same amount of water—see direction on the can.
2   Squeeze the juice of the whole lemon and grate the rind from half of it. Add this to the consommé with the sherry and season with black pepper. Bring to just below boiling point.
3   Drain and flake the tuna fish and add to the soup. Allow it just to heat through, without boiling again.
4   Garnish the soup with croûtons if available, and chopped parsley. Serve with savoury sticks such as Twiglets or Gristicks.

Consommé with Pasta

Use any pasta shapes you have on hand to give body and texture to canned consommé. The smaller the pasta, the more quickly it will cook.

2 298-g (10½-oz) cans condensed
consommé
40 g (1½ oz) small pasta shapes
(stars, alphabet or shells)

freshly ground black pepper
1 carrot
Parmesan cheese and Gristicks to
serve

1   Heat the consommé and add the pasta. Simmer for about 10 minutes—test to check that the pasta is just tender. Season with black pepper.
2   Scrape and grate the carrot and scatter it over the soup just as you take it to the table. Grated Parmesan cheese and long, crunchy Gristicks add to the Italian illusion.

Chicken Curry Soup

This soup does demand a moment's last minute attention, but as long as the stock is not actually boiling when you add the eggs, nothing can go wrong.

1·5 l (2½ pts) chicken stock, or use
stock cubes
3 eggs

2 tsp curry powder
25 g (1 oz) toasted almonds (page
183)

1   Heat the chicken stock until just below boiling point.
2   Meanwhile, beat the eggs and the curry powder together.
3   When you are ready to serve, take the pan from the heat, pour the egg mixture into the soup, stir with a fork and taste for seasoning.
4   Pour the soup into a heated tureen and garnish with the toasted almonds.

Egg and Lemon Soup

2 298-g (10½-oz) cans condensed consommé	2 tbsp lemon juice
	salt
1 tbsp dry sherry	freshly ground black pepper
50 g (2 oz) rice	1 dsp chopped parsley to garnish
2 eggs	

1   Tip the consommé into a pan with an equal amount of water, and the sherry. Heat to boiling point.
2   Add the rice. Stir well to keep the grains separate, cover and simmer for 20 minutes.
3   Meanwhile beat the eggs with the lemon juice.
4   Remove the pan from the heat and beat in the egg mixture. The soup must not be boiling at this point, or the egg will curdle.
5   Season the soup with salt and pepper. Pour into a heated tureen and garnish with parsley.

Beetroot Soup

Here's a quick way to whizz preserved beetroot into an improvised version of Hungarian soup.

275-g (10-oz) jar of pickled beetroot in vinegar	300 ml (½pt) soured cream
	salt
1·5 l (2½pts) water	freshly ground black pepper
1 tbsp flour	sugar if needed

1   Thoroughly drain the beetroot and liquidize it or push it through a sieve. Put it in a saucepan with the water and bring it to the boil.
2   In a small bowl, mix the flour to a smooth paste with a table-spoon of water, pour on a little of the beetroot liquid from the pan, then pour it back into the pan. Stir and bring it to the boil again. Simmer for about 5 minutes.
3   Pour in most of the soured cream, reserving a little to garnish. Heat gently to just below boiling point. Season with salt and pepper, and a little sugar if necessary.
4   Pour into a heated tureen and garnish with swirls of the reserved soured cream.

Pink-ice Soup

If you have the cans ready chilled in the refrigerator, this soup can be made for instant serving. Otherwise, make it in the evening or morning before and leave it to become thoroughly chilled. Offer only as much of the suggested garnish as you have time for.

525-g (1 lb 3-oz) can tomato juice, chilled
425-g (15-oz) can consommé, chilled
300 ml (½pt) natural yoghurt, chilled
2 tbsp Worcestershire sauce

salt
freshly ground black pepper

For the garnish
3 large carrots
2 small onions
3 stalks celery
garlic croûtons (page 185)

1 To make the soup, whisk together the tomato juice, consommé, yoghurt and sauce and season well with salt and pepper. Chill until needed.
2 For the garnish, trim, scrape and grate the carrots. Peel the onions and cut them into rings. Wash and finely chop the celery.
3 Offer the garnishes in separate bowls, to be sprinkled on each serving.

Cheese Mousse

A smooth creamy topping decorated with glistening red or black lumpfish roe (mock caviare), and beneath that a most unusual combination of flavours.

425-g (15-oz) can consommé, chilled
100 g (4 oz) Danish Blue cheese
a pinch of cayenne pepper
freshly ground black pepper

150 ml (5 fl oz) soured cream
50-g (2-oz) jar Danish lumpfish roe
1 large lemon
1 tsp chopped parsley to garnish

1 Pour the consommé into a blender and crumble in the cheese. Blend them until smooth and season with a pinch of cayenne pepper and black pepper.
2 Pour the mixture into 6 individual ramekin dishes and leave in the refrigerator to set for about 30 minutes.
3 Dribble soured cream on top of each dish and sprinkle with red or black 'caviare'.
4 Cut the lemon into 6 wedges and garnish each dish with lemon and chopped parsley.

Eggs with Mock Caviare

Danish lumpfish roe, coloured red or black, has an aura of luxury—at a realistic price.

6 eggs
mayonnaise

50-g (2-oz) jar Danish black
lumpfish roe
80-g (2¾-oz) can shrimps

1 Hard-boil the eggs, allow them to cool, halve them and cut them lengthways. Arrange them on a flat serving dish.
2 Spoon a little mayonnaise over each egg half (the appearance is greatly improved if you pipe the mayonnaise, but this takes longer).
3 Carefully spoon the lumpfish roe on to one end of each egg, and arrange the shrimps beside it, so that the egg halves have a domino appearance, black at one end and pale pink at the other. Wholemeal bread and butter or buttered sliced rye bread go well with this.

Artichoke Mayonnaise

3 hard-boiled eggs
480-g (1 lb 1-oz) can artichoke
*   hearts*
250 ml (scant ½pt) mayonnaise
1 tbsp soured cream

1 tsp Dijon mustard
salt
freshly ground black pepper
cayenne pepper to garnish

1 Peel the hard-boiled eggs and slice them into rounds. If you do not have an egg slicer, cut the eggs into wedges for speed.
2 Drain the artichokes and toss them on crumpled kitchen paper to dry.
3 Mix the soured cream and mustard into the mayonnaise and season well.
4 Toss the artichokes in the mayonnaise, then turn them into a serving dish.
5 Garnish them with overlapping circles of hard-boiled egg, sprinkled with cayenne pepper.

Artichoke Hearts with Anchovies

One of my own favourites.

480-g (1 lb 1-oz) can artichoke
*   hearts*

1 small clove garlic
1 tsp fresh chopped chives

1 tsp fresh chopped parsley
250 ml (scant ½ pt) French dressing
freshly ground black pepper

50-g (1¾-oz) can anchovy fillets
8 Spanish green stuffed olives to
garnish

1 Drain the artichoke hearts and toss them on to crumpled kitchen paper to dry.
2 Peel and crush the garlic and put it in a lidded beaker. Add the chives and parsley and the French dressing, and shake well.
3 Toss the artichoke hearts in the dressing and put them on a serving dish. Grind some black pepper over them.
4 Drain the anchovy fillets and criss-cross them over the artichokes.
5 Slice the olives and arrange them in the trellis spaces. Serve with wholemeal bread and butter.

Calamari Salad

425-g (15-oz) can calamari (squid)
1 large onion
150 ml (¼ pt) French dressing
½ tsp dried oregano

1 tbsp chopped parsley
salt
freshly ground black pepper
black olives

1 Drain the fish.
2 Peel and thinly slice the onion into rings.
3 Stir or shake the oregano into the French dressing with most of the parsley, reserving a little to garnish.
4 Toss the calamari in the dressing, taste and season with salt, if necessary, and pepper. Chill the salad until ready to serve.
5 Turn the salad into a serving dish and garnish with the onion rings, the reserved parsley and black olives. Good with wholemeal bread and butter or with pitta bread.

Herring Salad

Most delicatessen shops sell rollmop herrings, fresh or bottled, that can be enlivened with a few colourful garnishes.

6 large or 12 small rollmops
1 large onion

2 canned pimentos
2 large pickled gherkins

1 Arrange the rollmop herrings in a shallow serving dish and moisten them with a little of the liquor.

2   Peel the onion and slice it into thin rings. Scatter these over the
    herrings.
3   Cut the pimentos into thin strips and arrange them in a lattice
    pattern, criss-crossing over the fish.
4   Cut the gherkins into thin slices and arrange one piece in the
    centre of each pimento diamond. Good with wholemeal bread
    and butter.

Smoked Oyster Kebabs

These luxury-tasting kebabs also make a very good savoury to
serve at the end of a meal. They can be grilling while you clear away
the pudding plates.

2 90-g (3½-oz) cans smoked   *6 rashers streaky bacon*
  oysters   *cayenne pepper*

1   Drain the oysters from the liquid.
2   Cut the rind from the bacon, cut each rasher into 3 or 4 pieces
    (you need the same number of bacon strips as oysters) and
    stretch them with the back of a knife.
3   Wrap each oyster in a piece of bacon and divide them between
    six skewers.
4   Grill the kebabs under a hot grill for 4–5 minutes, turning once,
    until the bacon is beginning to crisp. Sprinkle with just a pinch
    of cayenne pepper. You can serve them kebab-house style, with
    slices of hot pitta bread, or, if you like, with fingers of hot toast.

5

MAIN DISHES

All recipes serve 6 unless otherwise stated

Most of the recipes in this chapter can be prepared well within half an hour on the night. But each one could be at least partly prepared in advance, to save precious moments. Even if your preparation amounts to no more than getting out the chopping board and knives, bowls and pans you will need, and fitting the attachment to the mixer, it is all a help.

Do everything you can to make life easier for yourself. Take the recipe with you to read in the train or bus, check the various stages of the method until you know most of them almost by heart. Check that you have all the ingredients you need, or make a shopping list under a separate heading for each store so that you can quickly get in and out of the shops at lunchtime.

If you are using meat from the freezer, remember to take it out at least the evening before (depending on the size of the cuts) and leave it in the refrigerator to thaw. If you are buying fresh meat or offal for a dish that needs slicing, try to chill it before cutting it up—it is much easier to handle. Or go one stage further and slice the meat, skin and core the kidneys and leave them close-wrapped in the refrigerator.

If you are buying frozen fish during the day, remember to take at least two strong polythene bags that do not leak. Then the fish can be thawing while you are at the office or completing your errands, without that embarrassingly smelly drip, drip, dripping. In very hot weather, an insulated picnic bag is a great advantage.

If you will be cooking fish, meat or vegetables in foil parcels, try to find time to cut the foil into the right-sized pieces—or better still, make a point of keeping a stock of large and small foil squares always ready.

Assemble as many of your ingredients as possible. A neat row of cans, bottles and tools on the kitchen table is a welcoming sight when the bus was late. Get out the cans of fish, soup or vegetables, the bottles of sauce, chutney and vinegars, look out the herbs, spices and stock cubes you will need, and bring the bottles of 'cooking' wine and spirit into the kitchen.

Prepare any ingredients that will not come to any harm in the process. Grate, slice or chop cheese for toppings and garnishes, chop or slice green peppers, mushrooms and parsley and leave them each in covered containers in the refrigerator—little yoghurt pots or margarine tubs are ideal. Squeeze or grate the lemon, chop nuts for garnish, and make herb or other flavoured butters.

Weigh any dry ingredients that can be left ready—pasta, coconut and flour, for example. And check that you have all the things you need to serve *with* the main course. Really good fresh bread is as perfect an accompaniment as any, and ideal for all the casual, informal dishes we like to serve our family and friends. Rice and pasta are perfect to soak up the sauce in braised and casseroled dishes—more about just how to cook them on pages 120 and 126. And salad often strikes a perfect balance, particularly with a rather rich main dish. Try to make the salad dressing in advance and, if you can, wash and dry the salad vegetables. Leave them in a closed polythene bag in the refrigerator and they will emerge as fresh as a daisy.

Starting from Scratch

Salmon Trout or Salmon Baked in Foil

Bake the fish in a parcel of foil to trap all the juices and flavour, and serve it with a flourish.

1·5 kg (3½lb) salmon trout, or about 1 kg (2¼lb) middle cut of fresh salmon
100 g (4 oz) unsalted butter
salt
freshly ground black pepper
1 bay leaf

1 tbsp lemon juice
a few parsley stalks

For the sauce
150 ml (¼pt) double cream and 2 tbsp chopped parsley, or hollandaise sauce (page 175)

1 Measure a piece of foil large enough to enclose the fish in a loose parcel, with double-sealed edges on three sides. Rub half of the butter over the foil to within 5 cm (2 in) of the edges and sprinkle the buttered area well with salt and pepper.
2 Lay the fish close to the centre of the foil and dot with the remaining butter. Cover the fish with the bay leaf, a sprinkling of lemon juice and the parsley. Fold the foil over to enclose the fish.
3 Double-seal two of the edges, pressing a firm crease. Put your hand inside the parcel and puff it up to allow plenty of head-room above the fish. The fish will cook in the steam of this area. Double-seal the third side.
4 Place the foil parcel on a baking sheet in the centre of the oven at 180°C (350°F), Gas 4. Bake the salmon trout for 40 minutes and the middle cut of salmon, which is much thicker, for 50 minutes.
5 You can unwrap the fish in the kitchen, transfer it to a buttered and heated serving dish and pour off the juices to make the sauce. Pour them into a small pan, add the cream and stir well over a low heat to blend and thicken. Taste for seasoning and

add more if necessary. Stir in the parsley and serve the sauce separately.
6   Or you can make quick hollandaise sauce while the fish is cooking, and serve the fish straight from the foil at the table. Slash the top of the parcel with a sharp knife.

Salmon Cutlets in Cucumber Sauce

6 salmon cutlets
600 ml (1 pt) water
1 tbsp tarragon vinegar
salt
freshly ground black pepper
1 small onion
½ lemon

1 bay leaf
a few sprigs of parsley
75 g (3 oz) butter
1 small cucumber
1 tbsp fresh chopped tarragon or
*   parsley*

1   Arrange the salmon cutlets side by side in a well-buttered baking dish.
2   Put the 'court bouillon' ingredients into a pan—the water, vinegar, salt, pepper, peeled and sliced onion, sliced lemon, bay leaf and parsley—and bring to the boil. Simmer for 5 minutes, so that the liquid absorbs the flavours.
3   Strain the liquor over the fish, cover with a lid or foil and cook in the oven at 180°C (350°F), Gas 4, for 20 minutes. Test that the fish is cooked—it should feel firm when touched with the point of a knife.
4   While the fish is cooking, melt the butter in a small pan. Peel the cucumber, slice it in half lengthways and scoop out the seeds. Cut each strip in half again, then chop up the flesh. Sweat the cucumber in the butter for 10 minutes, then stir in the fresh herbs. Season the sauce with salt and pepper and serve it separately.

Trout with Almonds and Apples

The sharpness of apples combines particularly well with trout and the texture is perfect with whole, firm fish.

6 trout, cleaned, heads left on
75 g (3 oz) butter
2 medium-sized cooking apples

40 g (1½ oz) whole blanched
*   almonds*
freshly ground black pepper

1   Thaw the fish if it is frozen. Wash the trout and pat them dry. Heat the butter in a large frying-pan. Peel, core and thickly slice

the apples and fry them in the butter, carefully turning them once, until they are brown. Remove them with a draining spoon to a hot dish and keep them warm.

2   Add the almonds to the butter and fry them, shaking the pan, to brown them. Transfer them to the dish with the apples.

3   Season the trout well with pepper. Add a little more butter to the pan if necessary. Fry the trout over a medium heat for about 5 minutes. Carefully turn them over and fry on the second side for the same time.

4   Gently lift the trout to a heated serving dish, pour over them any butter left in the pan and arrange the apples slices on top. Scatter with the almonds.

Trout Poached in White Wine

6 trout, fresh or frozen, cleaned
   and heads left on
150 ml (¼pt) dry white wine
3 tbsp water
1 small onion
½ lemon
a few sprigs of parsley

salt
freshly ground black pepper
300 ml (½pt) single cream
15 g (½oz) butter (omit if using
   toasted almonds)
24 almonds, whole blanched or
   toasted (page 183)

1   Thaw the trout if they are frozen. Wash them. Arrange them in a large frying-pan or, if you have one, a fish kettle. Pour on the wine and water.

2   Peel and chop the onion, slice the lemon and break up the parsley sprigs (reserve enough parsley to garnish) and add them to the pan. Season with salt and pepper, and bring the liquor slowly to the boil. Strain any scum from the surface. Cover the pan—with foil if it is has no lid—and simmer very gently for 10–15 minutes, depending on the size of the trout.

3   Using 2 fish slices, lift the fish from the liquor, arrange them on a hot serving dish and cover them with foil. Keep them warm.

4   Strain the liquor, return it to the pan and increase the heat. Rapidly boil the liquor to reduce it in quantity by half.

5   Meanwhile, melt the butter in a small pan over a moderate heat and brown the almonds, shaking them once or twice. (If you have ready-toasted almonds, use them instead.)

6   Chop 1 tablespoon parsley and stir it into the reduced liquor. Stir in the cream and heat the sauce gently without boiling. Taste for seasoning and add more salt or pepper if needed.

7   Pour the sauce over the fish and scatter the almonds on top.

Trout Vinaigrette

6 trout, fresh or frozen, cleaned
  and heads left on
3 eggs
50 g (2 oz) butter
1 small onion

1 green pepper
150 ml (5 fl oz) soured cream
3 tbsp white wine vinegar
salt
freshly ground black pepper

1 Thaw the trout if they are frozen. Wash and dry them.
2 Hard-boil the eggs.
3 Heat the butter in a large frying-pan. Peel and slice the onion into rings. Trim and slice the green pepper into rings, discarding the seeds. Fry them over a moderate heat until tender. Remove the vegetable rings from the pan and keep warm.
4 Fry the trout in the same pan for about 5 minutes on each side until they are cooked and golden brown.
5 Carefully remove the trout to a heated serving dish, scatter with the onion and pepper rings and cover with foil to keep warm.
6 Peel and chop the hard-boiled eggs. Add three-quarters of the chopped egg to the butter remaining in the pan. Stir in the soured cream and wine vinegar and season with salt and pepper. Heat the sauce gently.
7 Pour the hot sauce over the fish and sprinkle with the reserved chopped egg.

Grilled Red Mullet with Fennel

A classic Provençale dish with the unforgettable smell of charred fennel, and the excitement of leaping flames—it's certainly a talking point.

about 1·35 kg (3 lb) red mullet or
  sea bass, cleaned (you can cook
  either large or small fish in this
  way)
handful of dried fennel stalks

olive oil
salt
freshly ground black pepper
about 4 tbsp brandy

1 Line the rack of the grill pan with foil and criss-cross some dried fennel stalks over it. Pre-heat the grill to hot.
2 Slash the fish with a sharp knife twice on each side. Brush the fish liberally with olive oil on both sides and season well with salt and pepper. Turn the grill down to moderate. Grill the fish until it is crisp and golden brown, turn it over and grill the other side. The time will of course depend on the size and thickness of

the fish—a total time of about 15–24 minutes. Test with a sharp knife to make sure the fish is cooked. If any red juices run, brush with more oil and continue cooking.
3   Put the brandy in a small pan and heat it while the fish is cooking.
4   Transfer the fennel stalks to make a bed on a heated serving dish and lay the fish on top. Pour on the heated brandy and set light to it. Bring the dish to the table at once, the flames leaping and the fennel charring.

Mullet with Black Olives

Grey mullet has firm flesh and a delicate flavour which should not be masked by strong sauces.

6 small grey mullet, cleaned	*salt*
6 tbsp olive oil	*freshly ground black pepper*
5 tbsp dry vermouth	*12 black olives*
1 bay leaf	*1 lemon cut into 6 wedges*

1   Wash the fish and put them in a shallow ovenproof dish. Pour on the oil and vermouth, add the bay leaf and season with salt and pepper. Bake the fish at 180°C (350°F), Gas 4, for 15–20 minutes.
2   Add the olives and cook for a further 5 minutes. Remove the bay leaf and serve from the same dish, garnished with lemon wedges.

Spiced Halibut Baked in Cream

6 halibut or other white fish steaks	*salt*
175 g (6 oz) mushrooms	*freshly ground black pepper*
butter	*12 tbsp double cream*
curry powder	

1   Cut 6 squares of foil large enough to wrap the fish loosely. Butter the foil well.
2   Place a piece of halibut on each square of foil. Thinly slice the mushrooms on top of the fish. Sprinkle each one with a good pinch of curry powder and season with salt and pepper.
3   Spoon the cream over the fish and wrap each one into a loose parcel, making double-fold 'seams' down each of the 3 open sides.

4 Put the parcels in a baking dish and bake at 190°C (375°F), Gas 5, for 20–25 minutes, according to the thickness of the fish.

Halibut au Poivre

6 halibut or other white fish steaks
salt
2 tbsp black peppercorns
1 tbsp flour
1 tbsp vegetable oil
50 g (2 oz) butter
6 tbsp dry vermouth
150 ml (¼ pt) double cream

1 Wash and dry the fish and season it with salt.
2 Crush the peppercorns, using a pestle and mortar, a rolling pin, or a wooden spoon in a bowl. Stir the flour into the crushed spice and coat both sides of the fish with it.
3 Heat the oil and butter together in a frying-pan and cook the fish over moderate heat for about 6 minutes on each side, until it is firm. Remove the fish to a heated serving dish.
4 Pour the vermouth into the pan, stir well and bring just to the boil. Pour in the cream and allow to heat. Taste and adjust the seasoning if necessary. Pour the sauce round the fish.

Turbot Gruyère

A spiced cheesy topping adds moisture to any dry white fish—it is good with halibut and cod steaks, too.

6 turbot steaks
olive oil
salt
freshly ground black pepper
3 tomatoes
1 green pepper
6 slices Gruyère cheese
paprika to garnish

1 Heat the grill to hot. Cover the rack of the grill pan with foil and brush it with olive oil.
2 Arrange the fish on the foil, brush them with oil and season them well with salt and pepper. Turn the heat down to moderate and grill the fish for 5 minutes on the first side.
3 Carefully turn the fish over, brush with more oil, season again and grill for a further 4–5 minutes.
4 Meantime, halve the tomatoes, brush them with oil and season them. Trim the pepper, discard the seeds, and cut it into 6 rings.
5 Place a slice of cheese on each fish steak and sprinkle it with paprika. Return to the heat until the cheese is brown and bubbly.
6 Transfer the fish to a heated serving dish.

7 Quickly grill the tomato halves and pepper rings and place
   them on each steak.

Sole Coral

The fish fillets are baked in foil in a creamy prawn sauce—a lovely
surprise as the parcels are unwrapped.

6 large fillets of dover sole (or   *salt*
   plaice)   *freshly-ground black pepper*
175 g (6 oz) prawns, thawed   *1 tsp fresh chopped parsley*
100 g (4 oz) button mushrooms   *150 ml (¼ pt) double cream*
butter

1 Cut 6 squares of foil large enough to enclose a fish fillet.
2 Lightly butter each piece of foil. Place a fillet of sole on each and
   divide the prawns between them.
3 Thinly slice the mushrooms and divide them between the parcels. Season each one well with salt and pepper and sprinkle
   with chopped parsley. Spoon the cream over each fish.
4 Seal each piece of foil securely into a loosish parcel, making
   double folds on all 3 open sides.
5 Put the parcels on a baking tray or in a baking tin and bake at
   180°C (350°F), Gas 4, for 25–30 minutes.
6 Arrange the foil parcels on a heated tray serving dish and bring
   them, steaming hot, to the table as they are. Buttered potatoes
   go well with this.

Plaice Fillets with Mushroom Sauce

6 plaice fillets   *325 g (12 oz) button mushrooms*
flour   *1 large clove garlic*
salt   *1 tsp lemon juice*
freshly ground black pepper   *150 ml (¼ pt) double cream*
100 g (4 oz) butter   *parsley sprigs to garnish*

1 Thaw the fish if it is frozen. Wash and dry the fillets and coat
   them in flour seasoned with salt and pepper.
2 Heat half the butter in a large frying-pan until it foams. Fry the
   fish over a moderate heat first on one side, then the other, until
   they are golden brown and firm. Transfer the cooked fish to a
   heated serving dish and keep it warm.
3 Meanwhile, melt the remaining butter in a small pan.
4 Trim and thinly slice the mushrooms. Peel and crush the garlic.

5 Gently cook the mushrooms and garlic in the pan for 5–6 minutes over a moderate heat. Add the lemon juice and cream and season with salt and pepper. Heat the sauce through gently.

6 Pour the sauce over the fish and garnish with parsley.

Plaice Wheels with Parsley Butter

12 plaice fillets
100 g (4 oz) parsley butter (page 170, or see below, step 1)
25 g (1 oz) butter
1 small onion

20-cm (8-in) piece cucumber
150 ml (5 fl oz) soured cream
1 tbsp chopped parsley
salt
freshly ground black pepper

1 Thaw fish if it is frozen. Wash and dry the fillets. Spread the parsley butter on to the skinned side of the fillets and roll them up, starting at the tail end. Secure each rolled fillet with a cocktail stick. (If you do not have ready-made parsley butter, spread the fish with butter then season it with parsley, salt and pepper.)

2 Lightly grease a shallow ovenproof dish and arrange the fillets. Cover the dish (use foil if it has no lid) and bake at 180°C (350°F), Gas 4, for 15–20 minutes, until the fish is tender.

3 Meanwhile, make the sauce. Heat the butter in a small pan.

4 Peel and chop the onion. Peel and chop the cucumber. Fry them over a moderate heat for about 6 minutes, until the onion is cooked and the cucumber 'runny'. Stir in the soured cream and most of the parsley and season with a little salt and plenty of pepper. Heat gently.

5 Pour the sauce over the fish. Remove the cocktail sticks and garnish with a sprinkling of parsley.

Plaice with Roman Sauce (See Plate 6)

6 fillets or 6 small whole plaice
1 lemon
freshly ground black pepper

For the sauce
75 g (3 oz) butter
4 spring onions
50-g (1¾-oz) can anchovy fillets
2 tbsp capers
1 tbsp chopped parsley

1 Thaw the fish if it is frozen, wash and dry it.

2 Cut 6 pieces of foil, each one large enough to wrap the fish

loosely. Lightly butter the foil, put a fillet or plaice on each piece and season with pepper.

3 Squeeze the juice of the lemon and sprinkle a few drops over each fish—using about half.

4 Fold up each piece of foil to make a loose parcel, double-sealing each edge. Put the foil parcels on a baking sheet or in a baking tin and cook at 180°C (350°F), Gas 4, for 25–30 minutes, depending on the thickness of the fish.

5 While the fish is cooking trim and chop the spring onions.

6 Just before the fish is cooked, melt the butter in a small pan and fry the onions over a moderate heat for 1–2 minutes to soften them without browning.

7 Grate the rind of the lemon. Chop or finely cut the anchovy fillets and add them to the butter with the capers, lemon rind and reserved lemon juice.

8 When the fish is cooked, slit open each parcel, pour the sizzling hot sauce over each one, sprinkle with parsley and serve in the foil.

Sautéed Scallops with Mushrooms

18 large scallops	50 g (2 oz) butter (or ready-made
flour	garlic butter, page 171)
1 large clove garlic (omit if using	175 g (6 oz) button mushrooms
garlic butter)	1 dsp lemon juice
3 large spring onions	salt
6 tbsp olive oil	freshly ground black pepper
	1 tsp chopped parsley

1 Thaw the scallops if necessary. Wash and dry them. Cut each one into 3 pieces and toss them in flour.

2 Peel and finely chop the garlic. Trim, peel and slice the spring onions.

3 Heat the oil and butter together in a frying-pan.

4 Trim and thickly slice the mushrooms and turn them in the fat, over a moderate heat. Remove the mushrooms with a draining spoon and keep them warm.

5 Tip the scallops into the pan, stir them well and cook them over a moderate heat for 4–5 minutes until they firm up and become golden brown. Transfer the scallops to keep warm with the mushrooms.

6 Fry the garlic and spring onions in the pan for 2–3 minutes until the onion softens.

7   Return the scallops and mushrooms to the pan, season with the lemon juice, salt and pepper and stir to mix well. Turn into a heated serving dish and sprinkle with the parsley.

Haddock Sandwich

Cubes of fish are baked between layers of sherry-flavoured paste.

1 kg (2¼ lb) haddock fillet, fresh or
* frozen*
2 large cloves garlic
225 g (8 oz) butter
225 g (8 oz) fresh breadcrumbs

10 tbsp dry sherry
½ tsp dried dill weed
salt
freshly ground black pepper
parsley sprigs to garnish

1   Thaw the fish if it is frozen. Skin, wash and dry it. Cut it into large cubes, about 3·5 cm (1½ in).
2   Peel and crush the garlic.
3   Melt the butter. Pour half of it into a bowl and mix in the garlic, breadcrumbs, sherry and herb and season with salt and pepper.
4   Spread half of this paste over a greased shallow ovenproof dish. Arrange the fish cubes on the paste and cover them with the rest. Pour the remaining melted butter over.
5   Bake at 180 °C (350 °C), Gas 4, for 20–25 minutes until the fish is cooked and the top golden brown. Garnish with parsley sprigs.

Anchovy Cod

6 cod steaks, fresh or frozen
olive oil
freshly ground black pepper
400-g (15-oz) can tomatoes
minced garlic
½ tsp dried thyme

a pinch of dried mixed herbs
salt
225 g (8 oz) cheese, grated
50-g (1¾-oz) can anchovy fillets
12 stuffed green olives

1   Thaw and dry the fish.
2   Line the rack of the grill pan with foil and brush it with oil. Pre-heat the grill to hot. Lay the cod steaks on the foil and brush them with oil. Season them with pepper. Turn the heat to moderate and grill the fish for 4–5 minutes on each side.
3   Drain the can of tomatoes.
4   When the fish is cooked, divide the drained tomatoes between the 6 steaks. Sprinkle them with minced garlic and the dried herbs and season them with salt and pepper. Sprinkle the grated cheese on top of the fish and grill until it is golden brown and bubbly.

5   Arrange the anchovy fillets on the cheese topping and grill just
    enough to heat them.
6   Slice the olives and dot them between the anchovies.

Golden Fish

900 g (2 lb) fresh or frozen cod or   40 g (1½ oz) butter
   haddock fillet   salt
2 medium-sized onions   freshly ground black pepper
2 red peppers   1 tbsp turmeric
1 green pepper   75 g (3 oz) desiccated coconut
15 g (½ oz) root ginger   600 ml (1 pt) milk

1   Thaw the fish if it is frozen. Skin, wash and dry it and cut it into
    thick strips.
2   Skin and slice the onions. Trim and chop the peppers, discard-
    ing the seeds. Bang the ginger (with something like a wooden
    rolling pin) to bruise it.
3   Heat the butter in a flameproof casserole.
4   Fry the prepared vegetables and the ginger in the butter over a
    moderate heat for about 4 minutes.
5   Season with salt and pepper, stir in the turmeric and continue
    cooking for a couple of minutes. Stir in two-thirds of the
    coconut.
6   Slowly pour in the milk, stirring, and bring to the boil.
7   Lay the fish on the sauce and cover the casserole. Simmer for 15
    minutes. Remove the ginger.
8   Meanwhile toast the remaining coconut lightly under a
    medium grill and scatter it over the fish.

Honeypot Fish

900 g (2 lb) cod fillet skinned, or 6   3 tbsp clear honey
   steaks   200 ml (good ¼ pt) water
salt   2 lemons
freshly ground black pepper   1 clove garlic
flour   25 g (1 oz) pine nuts or blanched
a pinch of ground coriander   flaked almonds
2 tbsp cooking oil   40 g (1½ oz) seedless raisins
1 tsp dried rosemary   a pinch of nutmeg

1   Thaw the fish if it is frozen. Wash the fish, pat it dry and flip it in
    flour seasoned with salt, pepper and a pinch of ground corian-
    der.

2   Heat the oil in a shallow flameproof serving dish an(
    over a moderate heat for about 4 minutes on each
3   Meanwhile make the sauce. Put the honey and wat
    pan. Squeeze and strain the juice of the lemons. Pe(
    the garlic. Add the lemon juice and garlic to the pan witn tne
    nuts, raisins and a pinch of nutmeg. Bring to the boil.
4   Pour the sauce over the fish and simmer for 5 minutes, while
    the fish absorbs the flavours.

Italian Honey-baked Cod

6 cod cutlets
400-g (15-oz) can tomatoes
2 tbsp lemon juice
3 tbsp clear honey
2 tsp tomato purée
2 tbsp water
½ tsp dried oregano

salt
freshly ground black pepper
1 medium-sized onion
1 green pepper
1 bay leaf
40 g (1½ oz) blanched almonds

1   Wash the fish. Grease a shallow ovenproof dish and arrange
    the cutlets in it.
2   Drain the juice from the can of tomatoes into a bowl and mix in
    the lemon juice, honey, tomato purée and water and season
    with the dried oregano, salt and pepper.
3   Peel and slice the onion into rings. Trim and slice the pepper
    into rings, discarding the seeds. Scatter the vegetable rings over
    the fish and add the tomatoes with the crumbled bay leaf. Pour
    the honey sauce over.
4   Cover the dish and bake at 190 °C (375 °F), Gas 5, for 25 minutes,
    basting the fish once or twice. Scatter with the almonds and
    return to the oven for a minute or two more to brown the nuts.

Fish Baked in Wine

There's a great deal to be said for one-pot cooking—cooking and
serving in the same dish.

900 g (2 lb) cod or haddock
olive oil
1 medium-sized onion
1 green pepper
227-g (8-oz) can tomatoes
salt

freshly ground black pepper
½ tsp oregano
1 bay leaf
6 tbsp dry white wine
6 wedges of 1 large lemon

1 Thaw the fish if it is frozen. Skin, wash and dry it and cut it into large slices.
2 Brush a shallow ovenproof dish with olive oil and arrange the fish on the base.
3 Peel and slice the onion. Trim and chop the pepper, discarding the seeds. Tip the tomatoes into a bowl and stir in the vegetables. Season them with salt, pepper and the oregano and pour over the fish. Add the bay leaf.
4 Pour on the wine and about 2 tablespoons olive oil.
5 Cover the dish and bake at 170°C (325°F), Gas 3, for about 20–25 minutes, until the fish is firm and just tender. Remove the bay leaf and serve with wedges of lemon.

Fish Provençale

900 g (2 lb) cod or haddock fillet	*salt*
25 g (1 oz) butter	*freshly ground black pepper*
1 medium-sized onion	*400-g (15-oz) can tomatoes*
175 g (6 oz) streaky bacon	*1 bay leaf*
1 green pepper	*½ tsp dried oregano*
1 tbsp flour	*2 tsp sugar*

1 Thaw the fish if it is frozen. Skin, wash and dry the fish and cut it into cubes.
2 Heat the butter in a frying-pan or flameproof dish.
3 Peel and slice the onion. Cut off the rind and cut the bacon into squares. Trim and chop the pepper discarding the seeds.
4 Fry them all in the butter while you toss the fish in flour seasoned with salt and pepper.
5 Toss the fish into the pan, stir well and fry for 3 minutes.
6 Tip in the tomatoes, add the bay leaf, oregano and sugar, stir, and bring to the boil. Cover the pan and simmer for about 15 minutes until the sauce has thickened. Taste for seasoning and add more if needed. Remove the bay leaf.

Poached Skate

Skate has plenty of in-built moisture, so will not dry up on you.

1·35 kg (3 lb) wing of skate	*salt and a few peppercorns*
150 ml (¼ pt) water	*75 g (3 oz) butter*
2 tbsp white wine vinegar	*1 green pepper*
1 lemon	*1 heaped tbsp capers*
1 small onion	*1 tbsp chopped parsley*
2 bay leaves	*2 stuffed green olives*

1   Wash the fish and cut it into 6 pieces. Put it in a large frying-pan and pour on the water and the wine vinegar.
2   Cut half of the lemon into slices. Peel and slice the onion and add these to the pan with the bay leaves, peppercorns and a good pinch of salt. Bring to the boil over a moderate heat. Cover the pan (with foil if it has no lid) and poach the fish for 15–20 minutes, until it is firm.
3   Lift the fish carefully from the pan and arrange it on a heated serving dish in 'pairs', each two wing pieces together forming a butterfly shape. Keep the fish warm while making the sauce.
4   Heat the butter in a small saucepan.
5   Trim the green pepper, discard the seeds and cut it into 6 strips. Fry these in the butter until just tender. Remove them and arrange two strips between each 'pair' of fish, for the butterfly body.
6   Continue heating the butter in the pan until it browns, strain in the juice of the remaining half lemon, and stir in the capers and parsley.
7   Chop each olive into 3 slices and arrange these for the 'heads'.
8   Pour the sauce over the fish and serve very hot.

Fast-cook Cuts of Meat

No matter how adventurous we like to be with our cooking, there are times when a prime cut of meat, simply cooked to perfection, is the answer. A well-hung piece of rump steak, grilled or fried just the way it should be, and served with ravigote butter; chump chops of lamb glistening with mint butter, or baby chickens served with a fresh herb sauce—they are all hard to equal.

The table below is a guide to grilling and frying times, though the exact time will depend on the thickness of the meat, and what is understood by the terms 'high' or 'moderate' heat in relation to individual appliances.

Pre-heat the grill or frying-pan—a heavy one is a must. Then seal the meat quickly on both sides for a couple of minutes at high heat and lower the temperature to moderate to finish the cooking. Turn the meat once during cooking, unless you are using a double-sided grill appliance (see note on express cookers below), and use blunt kitchen tools such as tongs, wooden spoons or a spatula to avoid piercing the meat.

RUMP OR FILLET STEAK

	Grilled or Fried		
	Rare	Medium	Well done
	minutes	minutes	minutes
2 cm (¾ in) thick	5	9	12–14
2·5 cm (1 in) thick	6	10	14–15
3·5 cm (1½ in) thick	9	12–14	17–19

CHICKEN

	Grilled	Fried (Sauté)
	minutes	minutes
Individual joints	20	25–30
Poussin, split	15–20	15–20

OTHER CUTS OF MEAT

	Grilled or Fried
	minutes
Lamb or veal chops or cutlets	12–15
Pork chops (cooked thoroughly)	15–20
Gammon rashers 1·5 cm (½ in) thick	12–16
Liver, very thin strips	2–3
1·5 cm (½ in) thick slices	6–8
Lambs' kidneys	6–8

EXPRESS COOKERS

Cooking times may be cut considerably when using a 'double-sided' grill cooker, such as the Moulinex express cooker and combination grill. Sample grilling times are: beef steak, 5–10 minutes; lamb chops, 10–12 minutes; pork chops, 12–15 minutes; liver slices, 3 minutes; kidney, 3 minutes. Follow the times recommended by the manufacturer of each appliance.

Noughts and Crosses Steak

about 1 kg (2¼ lb) rump steak   *paprika pepper*
freshly ground black pepper   *50-g (1¾-oz) can anchovy fillets*
butter   *6 stuffed green olives*
100 g (4 oz) Gruyère cheese

1   Pre-heat the grill to high. Cut the steak into 6 pieces. Snip cuts along the fat to prevent it from curling up. Season the steaks well on both sides with the pepper and dot with butter. Put the steaks on the rack of the grill pan and grill each side for 2

minutes. Turn the heat to moderate and continue cooking the steaks for a further 3–6 minutes on each side, depending on the thickness of the steaks and how well you like them cooked.

2 Meanwhile, slice the cheese very thinly. (A hard cheese such as Gruyère slices very easily on a mandolin cutter, but of course a sharp knife will do.)
3 Arrange the cheese to cover the steaks, sprinkle with paprika pepper and return to the grill until the cheese has melted and is brown.
4 Transfer the steaks to a heated serving dish. Criss-cross anchovy fillets over each one and arrange sliced olives at each corner.

Steak with Mustard Cream

6 fillet steaks
1 clove garlic
salt
freshly ground black pepper
100 g (4 oz) butter
175 g (6 oz) button mushrooms

6 tbsp dry white wine
3 tbsp brandy
2 tbsp Meaux mustard
150 ml (¼ pt) double cream
parsley sprigs to garnish

1 Peel the garlic clove and cut it in half. Rub the steaks on both sides with the garlic and season them with salt and pepper.
2 Heat 75 g (3 oz) of the butter in a large, heavy frying-pan and when it is frothy, sear the steaks over a high heat, first one side and then the other. Lower the heat and finish cooking the steaks turning them once, for 8–15 minutes, depending on the thickness of the meat and the degree of cooking you prefer. Transfer the steaks to a heated dish, cover them with foil and keep them warm.
3 Add 25 g (1 oz) butter to the pan and heat it. Lightly fry the trimmed whole mushrooms for 1–2 minutes, shaking the pan so they are well coated with the butter. Remove them with a draining spoon and keep them warm with the steaks.
4 Pour the white wine into the pan and stir well with a wooden spoon to take up the juices. Add the brandy and the mustard, stir well, then add the cream. Season with salt and pepper. Heat without allowing the sauce to boil.
5 Arrange the steaks on a heated serving dish, with the mushrooms on top. Pour off any juices into the cream sauce, stir, and pour the sauce over the steak. Garnish with parsley sprigs.

Fried Steak with Anchovy Butter

If anchovy butter is one of your home-made stand-bys, this really is a meal in moments. If not, it will only take a couple of minutes to make.

50-g (1¾-oz) can anchovy fillets
  (unless anchovy butter used)
1 tsp strained lemon juice
175 g (6 oz) softened unsalted
  butter (or anchovy butter, page 171)

1 kg (2¼lb) sirloin steak
olive oil
freshly ground black pepper
chopped parsley to garnish

1 First make the anchovy butter so that it can rest in the refrigerator at least while you cook the steak. Drain the anchovy fillets from the oil in the can and pound them to a paste with the strained lemon juice. (If you have a blender, cut the anchovies in small pieces and reduce them to a paste with the lemon juice.) Beat the anchovy paste into the butter until it is smooth and thoroughly blended. If you do not have an electric mixer to do the beating, use a wooden spoon and settle for a slightly less-perfect blending. Shape the anchovy butter into a roll, wrap it in foil and leave in the refrigerator until needed.

2 Cut the steak into 6 pieces and snip the fat at intervals to prevent it from curling up as it cooks. Grind pepper on to both sides of the steak.

3 Heat a large, heavy frying-pan over high heat until the pan is very hot (hold your hand above it, or shake drops of water on the surface. They should sizzle and evaporate immediately). Brush the pan with a little olive oil. Put the steaks in the pan, sear them for 2 minutes, flip them over and sear the second side for 2 minutes. Reduce the heat under the pan and continue cooking the steaks, for about 4, 6 or 8 minutes on each side, depending on the thickness of the meat and whether you like them rare, medium or well-cooked. Transfer the steaks to a heated serving dish.

4 Cut the roll of anchovy butter into slices (any remaining will keep well in the refrigerator) and put one on top of each steak. Sprinkle with parsley and serve at once, very hot.

Steak with Ruby Sauce

6 fillet steaks
salt
freshly ground black pepper

ground bay leaves
50 g (2 oz) butter
6 tbsp red wine

4 tbsp port   *sprigs of parsley to garnish*
150 ml (¼pt) double cream

1   Season the steaks well with salt and pepper and rub them with
    a pinch of ground bay leaves.
2   Heat the butter in a large frying-pan until it is foaming, then
    cook the steaks over a high heat first on one side, then the other.
    Lower the heat to moderate and continue cooking the steaks for
    8–15 minutes turning them once. The time will depend on the
    thickness of the meat and how 'rare' or well-cooked you like it.
    Remove the steaks to a heated dish, cover them with foil and
    keep them warm.
3   Pour in the red wine and the port and stir well with a wooden
    spoon, scraping up all the juices from the pan. Bring the liquor
    to the boil, add the cream and heat without boiling. Taste and
    season with salt and pepper.
4   Arrange the steaks on a heated serving dish. Pour off any juices
    into the sauce, stir well and pour the sauce over the steaks.
    Serve garnished with parsley sprigs.

Chinese Pepper Steak

If the meat is cut really thinly, it is cooked in not much more than 5
minutes.

675 g (1½lb) rump steak   *freshly ground black pepper*
5 tbsp vegetable oil   *½tsp ground ginger*
1 large clove garlic   *1 rounded tbsp cornflour*
3 spring onions   *150 ml (¼pt) beef stock*
2 green peppers   *2 tsp soy sauce*
salt   *2 tbsp red wine*

1   Use a cleaver (page 16) or a very sharp knife with a straight or
    scalloped edge, to cut the meat. Cut it diagonally into very thin
    slices, about 1·5 cm (½in) thick, then cut the slices into match-
    stick lengths.
2   Heat the oil in a heavy frying-pan.
3   Peel and finely chop the garlic clove. Peel, trim and chop the
    spring onions. Trim and chop the green peppers, discarding the
    seeds.
4   Fry the meat in the hot oil, stirring, for about 3 minutes, until it
    browns. Add the garlic, spring onion and green pepper, season
    with salt, pepper and the ground ginger, and stir-fry for about
    2–3 minutes.
5   Put the cornflour in a cup, gradually mix in the stock, add the

soy sauce and red wine and pour into the pan. Bring to the boil, stirring over a high heat, and stir until the sauce thickens. Transfer to a heated serving dish.

Soured Cream Steak

The more thinly you cut the steak, the faster it will cook.

900 g (2 lb) sliced beef topside
salt
freshly ground black pepper
40 g (1½ oz) butter
15 g (½ oz) flour
2 tsp paprika

½ tsp mustard powder
250 ml (scant ½ pt) meat stock, or
  use stock cube
150 ml (5 fl oz) soured cream
1 tbsp chopped parsley

1   Using a very sharp knife, trim the meat and cut it into very thin strips, so that it will cook quickly. Season it with salt and pepper.
2   Heat the butter in a large pan and fry the meat, stirring it to brown on all sides. Cover the pan and simmer for 10 minutes.
3   Stir in the flour, paprika and mustard. Then gradually pour on the stock. Bring to the boil and simmer, covered, for a further 10 minutes.
4   Stir in the soured cream, allow just to heat through, then stir in the parsley.

Beef Stroganoff

Perhaps the best-known example of all of a dish that, being made from a prime cut of meat, cooks quickly.

675 g (1½ lb) fillet steak
1 medium-sized onion
325 g (12 oz) button mushrooms
75 g (3 oz) butter

salt
freshly ground black pepper
300 ml (½ pt) soured cream
1 tbsp chopped parsley to garnish

1   Using a very sharp knife, with a straight or scalloped edge, cut the meat across the grain in slices about 1 cm (½ in) thick. Cut the slices into 5-cm (2-in) long strips.
2   Peel and finely chop the onion. Trim and slice the mushrooms.
3   Heat half the butter in a heavy frying-pan and fry the onions over medium heat for about 4 minutes, until they are soft. Add the mushrooms, stir well and fry them for 2–3 minutes. Remove the vegetables with a draining spoon and keep them warm.
4   Heat the rest of the butter in the pan and fry the steak over a fairly high heat for 3–4 minutes, stirring to brown it on all sides.

The meat for this dish should be only lightly cooked, but how lightly is a matter of taste.

5   Lower the heat, return the vegetables to the pan, season with salt and pepper and stir in three-quarters of the soured cream. Allow the sauce to heat without boiling. Turn the meat into a heated serving dish. Spoon the reserved soured cream on top and garnish with the chopped parsley.

Fondue Bourguignonne

If you have one or two good sauces in hand, this is a good way to serve a meal quickly.

900 g (2 lb) sirloin steak
450 ml (¾pt) vegetable oil
salt
freshly ground black pepper

cold sauces to serve, e.g.
  mayonnaise, mustard
  mayonnaise, tomato
  mayonnaise, barbecue sauce,
  hot relish sauces (see Sauces,
  pages 173–83)

1   Cut the meat into 1-cm (½-in) cubes.
2   To save time, heat the oil in a small pan on the cooker, and pour it into the dish of a fondue set or, if you don't have a special one, a small flameproof casserole. Put the pan of oil over the fondue burner, or a candle-burning hotplate.
3   Provide each guest with a skewer and his share of the meat. Have bowls of salt and ground black pepper, and as many cold sauces as you can muster. Flavoured mayonnaise is particularly good.
4   The guests spear a piece of meat and hold it in the hot oil to cook, rare, medium or well done, to their liking, then dip the meat in the seasonings and sauces. Serve plenty of French bread, and perhaps a salad.

Bacon Ratatouille (See Plate 7)

Crispy bacon contrasts well with the medley of colourful vegetables.

300 g (10 oz) streaky bacon
50 g (2 oz) butter
1 large onion
2 cloves garlic
2 green peppers
2 tomatoes

450 g (1 lb) courgettes
50 g (2 oz) mushrooms
salt
freshly ground black pepper
5 ml (1 tsp) dried thyme
30 ml (2 tbsp) tomato purée

1   Derind and chop the bacon.
2   Melt the butter in a pan and fry the bacon until crisp. Remove and set aside.
3   Peel and chop the onion. Peel and crush the garlic.
4   Trim, deseed and slice the peppers. Peel and slice the tomatoes.
5   Wash, trim and slice the courgettes. Chop the mushrooms.
6   Fry the onion in the pan for about 3 minutes, then add the other vegetables. Stir well and fry for 5 minutes. Add the seasoning, thyme and tomato purée, stir and cover the pan. Simmer gently for 30–35 minutes until the vegetables are tender but not mushy. Stir in the bacon just before serving.

Crispy hot bread rolls are a lovely accompaniment.

Pork Chops with Raisin Sauce

6 pork chops
vegetable oil
salt
freshly ground black pepper
grated nutmeg

For the sauce
15 g (½ oz) butter

1 small onion
1 large orange
450 ml (¾ pt) chicken stock, or use stock cube
50 g (2 oz) seedless raisins
2 tsp cornflour
1 tbsp Worcestershire sauce

1   Snip the fat all round the chops to preserve the shape. Brush the meat with oil and season it well with salt, pepper and a pinch of grated nutmeg. Pre-heat the grill and grill the chops for 7–10 minutes on each side, until they are well cooked. Transfer them to a heated serving dish and keep warm.
2   Meanwhile, make the sauce. Heat the butter in a small saucepan. Peel and finely chop the onion and fry it for 4–5 minutes over a medium heat, until it is soft.
3   Squeeze and strain the juice and grate the rind of the orange and add these to the pan with the chicken stock and raisins. Bring the sauce to the boil and simmer for 10 minutes.
4   Stir the Worcestershire sauce into the cornflour to make a smooth paste, then stir it into the pan. Taste for seasoning and add salt and pepper. Bring to the boil again, stirring, and simmer until the sauce clears and thickens. Serve the sauce separately, in a heated sauceboat.

Pork in Orange Sauce

Cooks while you eat the first course.

900 g (2 lb) pork fillet
175 g (6 oz) button mushrooms
1 small onion
1 rounded tbsp flour
1 tsp ground coriander
salt
freshly ground black pepper

1 tbsp vegetable oil
40 g (1½ oz) butter
3 tbsp dry vermouth
5 tbsp fresh orange juice
150 ml (¼ pt) double cream
parsley sprigs to garnish

1 Trim any fat from the pork and cut the meat into slices about 2 cm (¾ in) thick.
2 Trim and slice the mushrooms. Peel and slice the onion.
3 Put the flour and coriander into a polythene bag, season with salt and pepper and toss in the meat. Shake to cover it thoroughly.
4 Heat the oil and butter together in a large pan and fry the pork over a moderate heat to brown it all over. Remove it to a heated dish to keep warm.
5 Fry the onion lightly in the pan, tip in any remaining flour and stir well to take up the juices. Pour in the vermouth and orange juice, stir and bring the sauce to the boil.
6 Return the pork to the pan with the mushrooms, stir, cover and leave to simmer over a low heat, stirring once or twice, for 20–25 minutes, until the meat is tender.
7 Stir in the cream and heat through without boiling. Turn the pork into a heated serving dish and garnish with the parsley.

Pork in Brandy Cream Sauce

about 1 kg (2¼ lb) pork fillet
salt
freshly ground black pepper
1 tsp dried rosemary
2 tbsp vegetable oil

25 g (1 oz) butter
2 tbsp brandy
1 tbsp orange liqueur (or wine)
4 tbsp double cream
1 tsp chopped parsley

1 Slice the pork into rounds about 3 cm (just over 1 in) thick and season them with salt, pepper and crumbled rosemary.
2 Heat the oil and butter together in a large frying-pan and seal the meat over a high heat for about 3 minutes on each side. Lower the heat, cover the pan and cook for a further 10 minutes, turning the meat once to cook it evenly. Transfer the meat to a heated serving dish and keep it warm.

3   Pour the brandy and orange, liqueur or wine into the pan and thoroughly stir all over the surface with a wooden spoon.
4   Spoon in the cream, stir well and heat it without boiling. Pour the sauce over the pork and garnish with sprinkled parsley.

Pork in Rum and Orange Sauce

Rum and orange might sound more like a drink of days gone by, but it's good with medallions of pork.

1 kg (2¼ lb) pork fillet	*salt*
3 large oranges	*freshly ground black pepper*
flour	*2 tbsp dark rum*
40 g (1½ oz) butter	*4 tbsp double cream*

1   Trim the pork fillets and cut them into rounds about 3 cm (just over 1 in) thick. Toss them in seasoned flour to coat them.
2   Squeeze the juice and grate the rind of 2 oranges. Slice the third one.
3   Heat the butter to foam in a large frying-pan over a fairly high heat. Add the pork and seal first one side, then the other. Cover the pan, lower the heat to moderate and continue cooking for about 10–12 minutes, turning the meat once during this time. Remove the pork to a heated serving dish and keep it warm.
4   Add the strained orange juice, the orange rind and the rum to the juices in the pan. Stir well and add the cream. Allow it just to heat, then pour the sauce over the pork. Garnish the dish with the slices of fresh orange.

Lamb Chops in Horseradish Sauce

After the initial preparation, you can leave the dish cooking while you begin the meal.

6 lamb chops	*1 tbsp horseradish sauce*
salt	*1 small carton yoghurt*
freshly ground black pepper	*75 g (3 oz) cheese, grated*
lemon juice	*2 heaped tbsp bran flakes*
50 g (2 oz) butter	

1   Season the chops with salt and pepper and sprinkle them with lemon juice.
2   Melt the butter in a frying-pan and fry the chops over a high heat for 3 minutes on each side. Transfer them to a heated baking dish.

3   Stir the horseradish sauce into the yoghurt and pour over the chops.
4   Stir the cheese and bran flakes together and sprinkle over the meat. Bake at 190°C (375°F), Gas 5, for 30 minutes, until the chops are tender.

Spiced Lamb Chops (See Plate 8)

6 lamb chops
50 g (2 oz) butter
200-g (7-oz) can apricots
50 g (2 oz) sultanas

1 tsp curry powder
salt
freshly ground black pepper

1   Melt the butter in a pan and fry the chops over a high heat for 3 minutes on each side. Lower the heat to medium and pour off the fat. Add the remaining ingredients, cover the pan and simmer gently for 30 minutes until the chops are tender, stirring occasionally.
2   Transfer the chops and the sauce, which should now be quite thick, to a heated serving dish.

Lamb Chops with Cheese Butter

6 chump-end lamb chops
175 g (6 oz) butter
1 tsp dried rosemary

salt
freshly ground black pepper
75 g (3 oz) Parmesan cheese

1   Melt half the butter in a flameproof baking dish and fry the chops over a high heat for 1 minute on each side. Remove the dish from the heat, sprinkle the chops with the rosemary, salt and pepper, and roast in the oven at 230°C (450°F), Gas 8, for 15 minutes, until the chops are tender, turning them once.
2   Meanwhile, beat the grated cheese into the rest of the butter, shape it into a roll and cut it into 6 pats.
3   Transfer the chops to a heated serving dish and divide the cheese butter between them.

Lamb Maryland

6 lamb chops
salt
freshly ground black pepper
50 g (2 oz) butter
1 tbsp vegetable oil
150-g (5-oz) can red pimentos

275-g (10-oz) can sweetcorn
   kernels
3 tbsp tomato purée
5 tbsp water
a pinch of sugar
2 bananas

1 Season the chops with salt and pepper.
2 Heat the butter and oil in a frying-pan and fry the chops over a moderate heat for 8 minutes on each side. Remove them to a heated serving dish and keep them hot.
3 Drain and chop the pimentos and add them to the pan with the drained sweetcorn, tomato purée and water. Season with salt and pepper and sugar. Stir well. Bring the sauce to the boil and simmer for 4–5 minutes.
4 Peel and chop the bananas and stir them into the sauce. Allow them to heat through, then pour the sauce over the chops.

Paprika Lamb Chops

6 lamb chops
50 g (2 oz) butter
1 large onion
1 clove garlic
1 tbsp tomato purée

1 tbsp paprika, salt
freshly ground black pepper
300 ml (½ pt) chicken stock, or use
 stock cube
1 bay leaf

1 Heat the butter in a large pan and fry the chops over moderate heat for 3 minutes on each side. Remove them to a heated dish to keep warm.
2 Meanwhile, peel and slice the onion and peel and crush the garlic. Add them to the pan after removing the chops and fry them for 5 minutes.
3 Add the tomato purée, paprika, salt and pepper, stir well and gradually pour on the stock. Return the chops to the pan, add the bay leaf, cover and simmer for 20 minutes, until the chops are tender. Remove the bay leaf.
4 Transfer the chops and sauce to a heated serving dish.

Lemon Veal

6 slices veal escalope (ask the
 butcher to flatten)
salt
freshly ground black pepper
2 tbsp olive oil

50 g (2 oz) butter
6 spring onions
2 small, thin-skinned lemons
6 tbsp dry vermouth
1 tbsp chopped parsley

1 Season the meat well on both sides with salt and pepper.
2 Heat the olive oil and butter together in a large heavy frying-pan over a fairly high heat and when it is frothy put in the meat. Seal the meat quickly on the first side.

3 Trim, peel and chop the onions. Thinly slice the lemon.
4 Flip the meat over to seal it on the second side. Lower the heat to moderate and add the onions and lemon slices. Cook for a few minutes until the meat is just tender, but still juicy.
5 Transfer the veal to a heated serving dish and keep warm.
6 Pour the vermouth into the pan. Sprinkle on the parsley and stir to take up all the pan juices. Taste for seasoning and add more if needed. As soon as the sauce is hot, pour it over the veal and serve.

Veal Rarebit

6 slices veal escalope (ask the
    butcher to flatten them)
2 peppers, 1 red, 1 green
100 g (4 oz) button mushrooms
100 g (4 oz) cooked ham
1 tbsp vegetable oil
75 g (3 oz) butter
25 g (1 oz) blanched almonds
salt
freshly ground black pepper
100 g (4 oz) Gouda cheese

1 Season the veal well with pepper.
2 Trim the red and green peppers, discarding the seeds, and cut into thin strips. Trim and slice the mushrooms. Cut the fat from the ham and cut the lean meat into thin strips.
3 Heat the oil and 25 g (1 oz) butter in a large frying-pan over a fairly high heat and when it is foaming add the veal. Quickly seal the meat on the first side, then flip it over to seal the second side. Turn the heat down to moderate and cook the veal, turning it once, for a further 10 minutes. Transfer the veal to the rack of a grill pan. Heat the grill.
4 Add the remaining butter to the fat in the pan and when it is hot tip in the prepared vegetables and the almonds. Stir well and fry for 4–5 minutes, then add the ham. Season with salt and pepper. Stir and just heat through.
5 Thinly slice the cheese and divide it between the 6 pieces of veal. Grill them until the cheese melts and bubbles.
6 Arrange the veal on a heated serving dish and garnish it with the vegetable mixture.

Rolled Veal Escalopes

It takes only moments to roll the escalopes and secure them with a cocktail stick, and ensures that the meat is juicy, with trapped-in flavour.

12 small veal escalopes (ask the
  butcher to flatten)
75 g (3 oz) Gruyère cheese
½ tsp dried rosemary
2 tsp pine nuts
salt
freshly ground black pepper

flour
50 g (2 oz) butter
4 tbsp meat glaze, use 'jelly' from
  beneath meat dripping, or
  condensed consommé
5 tbsp Marsala
sprig of rosemary to garnish

1   Grate the Gruyère cheese and mix it in a bowl with the crushed rosemary and pine nuts. Season the mixture with salt and pepper.
2   Divide the filling between the escalopes and roll them up, securing each one with a cocktail stick. Toss the rolls in flour.
3   Heat the butter in a large frying-pan and fry the veal rolls to brown them on all sides. Transfer them to a heated dish while you make the sauce.
4   Spoon the meat glaze and Marsala into the pan, stir well to take up all the pan juices, and bring the sauce to the boil. Return the veal to the pan, cover, and simmer over a very low heat for about 15 minutes, while you serve the first course.
5   Turn the veal into a heated serving dish. Garnish with a sprig of fresh rosemary, if available.

Veal Stroganoff

6 veal escalopes (ask the butcher to
  flatten)
2 medium-sized onions
1 clove garlic
325 g (12 oz) button mushrooms
50 g (2 oz) butter
2 tbsp vegetable oil

300 ml (½ pt) soured cream
1 tbsp tomato purée
1 tbsp French mustard
salt, 1 tsp paprika
freshly ground black pepper
1 tbsp chopped parsley

1   Using a very sharp knife, trim the meat and cut it into thin strips.
2   Peel and slice the onions. Peel and crush the garlic. Wipe and slice the mushrooms.
3   Heat the butter and oil in a frying-pan and fry the veal over moderate heat for 3 minutes, stirring once or twice, until it is evenly browned. Remove the veal with a draining spoon to a heated plate and keep warm.
4   In the same pan, fry the onions and garlic for about 5 minutes, stirring occasionally. Add the mushrooms and fry, stirring once or twice, for a further 3–4 minutes.

5   Mix together the soured cream, tomato purée, mustard, salt, pepper and paprika and pour into the pan. Stir and cook for 1–2 minutes, then return the veal to the pan, stir and heat through without allowing the sauce to boil.
6   Transfer to a heated serving dish and garnish with the chopped parsley.

Paprika Veal

6 veal escalopes (ask your butcher
*   to flatten)*
1 medium-sized onion
1 large clove garlic
50 g (2 oz) butter
2 tsp paprika

1 heaped tsp flour
1 orange
salt
freshly ground black pepper
150 ml (5 fl oz) soured cream

1   Peel and slice the onion. Peel and crush the garlic.
2   Heat the butter in a large frying-pan and fry the veal over a high heat for 2 minutes on each side. Lower the heat and cook the veal for a further 10 minutes. Remove the meat and keep it warm.
3   Fry the onion and garlic in the pan over a moderate heat until they are soft, stir in the paprika and cook for 2 minutes. Stir in the flour and cook for another 2 minutes.
4   Squeeze the juice and grate the rind of the oranges and strain into the pan. Season the sauce with salt and pepper and pour on the soured cream. Heat without boiling and check seasoning.
5   Return the veal to the pan and stir for a moment or two. Turn the meat on to a heated serving dish and garnish with a sprinkling of paprika.

Paprika Kidneys

Kidneys take a little time to prepare but they are conveniently quick to cook.

12 large lambs' kidneys
1 tbsp vegetable oil
50 g (2 oz) butter
1 small clove garlic
1 medium-sized onion
flour
salt
freshly ground black pepper

1 tsp paprika
½ tsp dried oregano
250 ml (scant ½ pt) chicken stock,
*   or use stock cube*
2 tbsp tomato purée
150 ml (5 fl oz) soured cream
1 tbsp chopped parsley

1   Skin and halve the kidneys, snip out the cores with very sharp kitchen scissors.
2   Heat the oil and butter together in a frying-pan.
3   Peel and crush the garlic. Peel and chop the onion. Sauté the garlic and onion in the fat, over a moderate heat, until the onion is soft and transparent but has not begun to brown. Remove with a draining spoon and keep warm.
4   Meanwhile, toss the kidneys in flour seasoned with salt and pepper.
5   When the onions are cooked, fry the kidneys in the pan until they are brown on both sides. Sprinkle on the paprika and dried herb, season with a little salt and pepper and pour on the stock, stirring. Stir in the tomato purée, cover the pan and simmer for 5 minutes.
6   Stir in 4 tablespoons of the soured cream and just heat through.
7   Stir in the parsley and turn into a heated serving dish. Swirl over the rest of the soured cream and sprinkle with a pinch of paprika.

Kidneys in Sherry

The sherry here enhances the flavour of the kidneys.

675 g (1½ lb) lambs' kidneys	*flour*
325 g (12 oz) button mushrooms	*salt*
4 tbsp olive oil	*freshly ground black pepper*
2 cloves garlic	*½ tsp dried oregano*
400-g (15-oz) can tomatoes	*6 tbsp dry sherry*

1   Skin the kidneys, halve them and remove the cores with a pair of sharp kitchen scissors.
2   Trim and thickly slice the mushrooms.
3   Heat 1 tablespoon olive oil in a saucepan. Peel and crush the garlic and fry in the oil for about 1 minute. Tip in the tomatoes and cook over a fairly high heat until the mixture dries. Beat with a wooden spoon to break up the tomatoes.
4   Meanwhile toss the kidneys in flour seasoned with salt and pepper and the dried herbs.
5   Heat the remaining 3 tablespoons oil in another pan, toss in the sliced mushrooms until they begin to soften, then remove them with a draining spoon and keep them warm.
6   In the same pan, fry the kidneys, stirring them with a wooden spoon to brown them on all sides.

7   Pour in the sherry, stir well, then add the tomato sauce and the mushrooms. Cover the pan and simmer over a low heat for 4–5 minutes. Turn the mixture into a heated serving dish.

Kidneys in White Wine

You need to be in the kitchen for about a quarter of an hour but once the dish is cooked it's quite good-tempered about being kept waiting.

12 large lambs' kidneys	freshly ground black pepper
1 tbsp vegetable oil	½ tsp dried thyme
75 g (3 oz) butter	150 ml (¼ pt) dry white wine
225 g (8 oz) button mushrooms	150 ml (¼ pt) chicken stock, or use
2 medium-sized onions	stock cube
1 rounded tbsp flour	1 dsp lemon juice
salt	parsley sprigs to garnish

1   Skin and halve the kidneys and snip out the cores with a pair of sharp kitchen scissors.
2   Heat the oil and half the butter together in a frying-pan.
3   Trim and slice the mushrooms and fry them for 3–4 minutes. Transfer them to a heated dish and keep warm.
4   Heat the remaining butter in the pan. Peel and chop the onions and fry them in the pan for 2–3 minutes. Transfer them to the dish with the mushrooms.
5   Add the kidneys to the pan and fry them until they are brown on both sides. Remove them, too, to the heated dish to keep warm.
6   Stir the flour into the fat in the pan and gradually pour on the wine and stock. Stir to blend well, season with salt, pepper and the dried herbs and bring to the boil. Simmer the sauce, uncovered, for 5 minutes.
7   Return the mushrooms, onions and kidneys to the pan, add the lemon juice and stir well. Cover and simmer for a further 5 minutes. Turn into a heated serving dish and garnish with parsley sprigs.

Calves' Liver with Sage Leaves

You need fresh, whole sage leaves to 'make anything' of this dish.

12 thin slices calves' liver, about
   675 g (1½ lb)
flour
salt
freshly ground black pepper
50 g (2 oz) butter

handful of fresh sage leaves
6 tbsp meat glaze, use 'jelly' from
   beneath meat dripping, or 12
   tablespoons chicken stock, or
   condensed consommé
1 tsp lemon juice

1 Put about 2 tablespoons of flour into a polythene bag, season it with salt and pepper and toss in the slices of liver to cover them.

2 Heat the butter in a large frying-pan and fry the liver over a fairly high heat for about 3 minutes on the first side. Toss in the sage leaves, flip over the liver and fry the second side until the liver is just firm, but tender.

3 Add the meat glaze to melt in the pan, stir well and add the lemon juice. Grind on some more pepper and transfer to a heated serving dish. If using meat stock, heat the stock in a small pan first over a high heat, until it is reduced by half. Then pour into the pan with the liver and stir well to take up the pan juices.

Liver with Madeira Sauce

675 g (1½ lb) sliced lambs' liver
1 tbsp olive oil
50 g (2 oz) butter
1 small onion
1 large clove garlic
flour

salt
freshly ground black pepper
a large pinch of grated nutmeg
1 orange
8 tbsp dry Madeira or sherry
2 tbsp chopped parsley

1 Heat the oil and butter together in a large frying-pan. Peel and chop the onion. Peel and crush the garlic. Fry them for 3–4 minutes over a low heat.

2 Coat the liver slices in flour seasoned with salt, pepper and nutmeg and cook them over a moderate heat, first on one side and then on the other until the liver is just tender—about 8 minutes, depending on the thickness. Remove the liver to a heated serving dish and keep it warm.

3 Meanwhile squeeze the juice and grate the rind of the orange.

4 Add the strained orange juice, the orange rind and the Madeira or sherry to the pan and stir well. Bring the sauce to the boil, add most of the parsley and heat through.

5 Pour the sauce over the liver and garnish it with the reserved parsley.

Liver in Soured Cream

about 675 g (1½lb) sliced calves'
   liver
1 tbsp vegetable oil
75 g (3 oz) butter
225 g (8 oz) button mushrooms
2 medium-sized onions

300 ml (½pt) soured cream
1 lemon
salt
freshly ground black pepper
1 tbsp chopped parsley

1 Cut the slices of liver slantways into 0·5-cm (¼-in) strips, then cut the strips into matchstick lengths.
2 Heat the oil and half the butter together in a frying-pan. Trim and slice the mushrooms and fry them for about 3 minutes over a moderate heat. Remove them with a draining spoon to keep warm.
3 Add the rest of the butter to the fat in the pan and when it foams tip in half the liver. Fry it, stirring, until it is just firm. Remove the liver and keep warm, cook the second half and transfer that to the warm dish.
4 Peel and chop the onions and fry them in the fat until they are soft.
5 Return the mushrooms and liver to the pan, add the soured cream and the strained juice and grated rind of the lemon, and season with salt and pepper. Stir well and allow to heat through. Stir in the parsley and turn into a heated serving dish.

Chinese Chicken and Peppers

6 chicken breasts or turkey
   portions
1 tbsp cornflour
2 tbsp soy sauce

5 tbsp vegetable oil
4 green peppers
1 large clove garlic
2·5-cm (1-in) fresh ginger root

1 Cut the chicken into pieces about 2·5 cm (1 in) square. Put them in a bowl and sprinkle on the cornflour. Shake well to coat the chicken pieces, then pour on 1 tablespoon of soy sauce and 1 tablespoon vegetable oil. Stir and leave to stand, even for a few minutes.
2 Trim the green peppers, discarding the seeds. Cut the flesh into slightly smaller squares than the chicken.

3   Peel and crush the garlic. Thinly slice the ginger.
4   Heat the remaining 4 tablespoons oil in a heavy frying-pan. Tip
    in the green peppers and stir-fry (page 133) over a moderate
    heat for 2–3 minutes until they are barely tender. Remove the
    peppers with a draining spoon and keep them warm.
5   Increase the heat under the pan and let the oil become very hot.
    Fry the crushed garlic and sliced ginger for a few seconds and
    then discard them. Stir-fry the drained chicken pieces for about
    4 minutes until they are golden brown.
6   Return the peppers to the pan, sprinkle on 1 tablespoon soy
    sauce and stir well. Turn into a heated serving dish.

St. Clement's Chicken (See Plate 8)

6 chicken joints	1 tbsp lemon juice
2 medium-sized onions	salt
1 large clove garlic	freshly ground black pepper
2 oranges	a pinch of ground coriander
2 tbsp vegetable oil	1 tbsp sugar
2 tsp turmeric	2 tsp cornflour
750 ml (1¼ pts) chicken stock, or	
use stock cubes	

1   If you have time, skin the chicken joints and prick the flesh all
    over with a large darning needle. This improves the flavour, but
    is not essential.
2   Peel and slice the onions. Peel and crush the garlic. Slice the
    oranges.
3   Heat the oil in a large frying-pan and fry the onions and garlic
    for 3–4 minutes over moderate heat.
4   Add the chicken joints and fry for 10 minutes, turning them so
    that they are browned on all sides.
5   Stir in the turmeric and gradually pour on the chicken stock and
    lemon juice. Bring the sauce to the boil and season with salt,
    pepper, sugar and a pinch of ground coriander.
6   Add the orange slices, cover the pan and simmer over a fairly
    low heat for 15 minutes.
7   Blend the cornflour with a little water to make a smooth paste.
    Pour it on to the chicken, stir well and increase the heat to bring
    the sauce to the boil again. Boil for 2 minutes. Turn the chicken
    into a heated serving dish.

Noodles with Ham and Cream Sauce

450 g (1 lb) noodles
75 g (3 oz) butter
1 tbsp vegetable oil
1 large onion
1 clove garlic
225 g (8 oz) button mushrooms

225 g (8 oz) cooked ham
2 egg yolks
150 ml (¼ pt) double cream
salt
freshly ground black pepper
1 tbsp chopped parsley

1   Cook the noodles in plenty of boiling, salted water in an uncovered pan, until they are just tender—follow the directions on the packet for the exact cooking time. Drain the noodles into a colander, refresh them with cold, running water and drain well.
2   Melt 25 g (1 oz) of the butter in the pan and gently reheat the noodles over a low heat. Keep them warm.
3   Meanwhile, prepare the vegetables. Peel and slice the onion. Peel and crush the garlic. Wipe and slice the mushrooms. Cut the ham into thin strips.
4   Heat the butter and oil in a pan, gently fry the onion and garlic for 5 minutes, add the mushrooms and cook for a further 3 minutes, then add the ham. Stir well and allow it to heat through.
5   Beat the egg yolks and cream together and season with salt and pepper.
6   Turn the noodles into a heated serving dish, pour on the cream sauce and toss well, using two spoons. Pour on the ham mixture and garnish with the parsley.

Noodles with Courgette Sauce

450 g (1 lb) green noodles
75 g (3 oz) butter
2 tbsp vegetable oil
2 large onions
1 clove garlic
450 g (1 lb) courgettes

400-g (15-oz) can tomatoes
1 tsp dried oregano
salt
freshly ground black pepper
50 g (2 oz) Parmesan cheese

1   Cook the noodles in a large, uncovered pan in plenty of boiling, salted water, following the directions on the packet. Drain them in a colander, refresh and separate them under cold, running water and drain again. Gently reheat them in a pan with half of the butter, and keep them warm.
2   Meanwhile, peel and slice the onions. Peel and crush the garlic.

Trim the courgettes and cut them slantwise into 1-cm ($\frac{1}{2}$-in) chunks.

3   Melt the remaining butter and the oil in a pan and fry the onion and garlic over moderate heat for 5 minutes, stirring once or twice. Add the courgettes, cover the pan and simmer for 10 minutes, shaking the pan once or twice. Tip in the tomatoes, add the herb and seasoning and stir well. Bring just to simmering point.

4   Put a layer of the vegetable mixture in a greased, ovenproof serving dish, then a layer of pasta and so on, finishing with the vegetables. Sprinkle the cheese on top. You can complete the dish to this stage just before the meal, and keep it warm.

5   While you are eating the first course, put the dish under the grill until the cheese bubbles and is golden brown.

Cheese Fondue

550 g (1¼ lb) Gruyère or   *freshly ground black pepper*
*   Emmenthal cheese*   *a large pinch nutmeg*
2 rounded tbsp flour   *25 g (1 oz) butter*
450 ml (¾ pt) dry white wine   *150 ml (¼ pt) double cream*
1 large clove garlic   *4 tbsp Kirsch or brandy*
salt   *French bread to serve*

1   Grate the cheese and mix it with the flour.
2   Put the wine in a small pan with the peeled and halved garlic clove. Bring the wine to the boil and boil until it is reduced to three-quarters of the volume. Remove the garlic and pour the wine into a flameproof casserole or fondue dish over a pan of hot water.
3   Gradually stir in the cheese and when it has all melted, season it well with salt, pepper and nutmeg.
4   Add the butter and half the cream, stir, and when it has blended stir in the remaining cream and the Kirsch or brandy.
5   Cut French bread into small cubes.
6   Call everyone to the table! Stand the dish on a fondue burner or candle-burning hotplate. Provide each guest with a skewer, and plenty of bread cubes within reach. Each person spears the bread and dips it into the fondue.

A green salad is refreshing after this rich, cheesy, creamy mixture. Or you could serve fresh fruit.

Cheesemonger's Flan

225-g (8-oz) pack shortcrust
   pastry
2 tbsp tomato ketchup
125 g (5 oz) Samsoe cheese
1 small onion
50 g (2 oz) fresh brown
   breadcrumbs

2 eggs
1 tsp mustard powder
1 tbsp milk
salt
freshly ground black pepper
a pinch of mixed dried herbs
a few whole blanched almonds

1 Roll out the pastry on a floured board and line a 20-cm (8-in) non-stick flan ring on a non-stick baking sheet. Trim the pastry, and if you have time re-roll the trimmings and cut them into long strips ready to make a criss-cross pattern on top of the flan.
2 Spread the tomato ketchup on the base of the flan case.
3 Grate the cheese. Peel and grate the onion. Make the breadcrumbs.
4 Mix together the grated cheese, the onion and the breadcrumbs.
5 Beat the eggs and pour them into the cheese mixture with the mustard powder and milk. Season well with salt and pepper and the dried herbs. Pour the filling into the flan case.
6 If you have made the pastry strips arrange them over the top of the flan and put an almond in each square. Otherwise, scatter the almonds on top of the filling. Brush the edge of the flan, and the top, with milk.
7 Bake at 200°C (400°F), Gas 6, for 25 minutes whilst preparing the first course. Serve hot.

With a Little Forethought

Whether it is simply marinating meat or fish in a medley of oil, wine and herbs and leaving them to impart their succulence and flavour, or coating meat in a crunchy cloak, it is comforting to know that some, at least, of the preparation—and the washing-up—is behind you.

Chinese Grilled Fish

6 small plaice or dabs
4 tbsp soy sauce
8 tbsp vegetable oil
8 tbsp water
6 tbsp dry sherry
freshly ground black pepper

For the sauce
3 tbsp soy sauce
6 tbsp vinegar
150 ml ($\frac{1}{4}$ pt) water
2 tbsp honey
6 tbsp dry sherry
1 tbsp sugar
1 tbsp cornflour
6 wedges of lemon to garnish

1 Wash the fish and arrange them in a single layer on a large dish or plate.
2 Mix together the soy sauce, oil, water and sherry. Season well with pepper and pour the basting sauce over the fish. Leave them to marinate for 30 minutes if possible.
3 Meantime, line the rack of the grill pan with foil and heat the grill.
4 Grill the fish under a medium heat, basting from time to time, until it just flakes when pushed with a knife blade.
5 While the fish is cooking, make the sweet and sour sauce. In a small pan, mix together the soy sauce, vinegar, water, honey, sherry and sugar. Bring to the boil.
6 Mix the cornflour to a smooth paste with a little water and pour it into the pan. Bring the sauce back to the boil and simmer for 2 minutes, stirring.
7 Transfer the fish to a heated serving dish and garnish them with wedges of lemon. Serve the sauce separately.

Fish Kebabs

If you do not have time to cut up the fish and marinate it
in the sauce baste it more frequently as it cooks.

900 g (2 lb) thick end of cod fillet, skinned	1 tbsp chopped parsley
8 tbsp olive oil	salt
2 tbsp clear honey	freshly ground black pepper
2 lemons	6 medium-sized tomatoes
2 bay leaves	6 very small onions
	100 g (4 oz) button mushrooms

1 Wash and dry the fish. Cut it into cubes about 3·5 cm (1½ in) square. Roll up any 'trimmings' to make more chunks.
2 Put the olive oil and honey into a shallow dish. Squeeze and strain the juice of both lemons and grate the rind of one over the dish. Crumble in the bay leaves, add the parsley and season well with salt and pepper. Mix the marinade with a fork.
3 Toss the fish in the marinade. Either cover and leave in a cold place, turning the fish once or twice, or cook straight away.
4 Quarter the tomatoes. Peel the onions and break them into sections. Trim the mushrooms.
5 Pre-heat the grill to hot and line the rack of the grill pan with foil.
6 Brush 6 kebab skewers with oil. Divide the fish and prepared vegetables equally and thread them on the skewers.
7 Arrange the skewers on the grill pan. Brush them with half of the marinade. Reduce the heat to moderate and grill the skewers for 5 minutes, basting with the marinade. Turn them over and pour on the remaining marinade. Grill them for a further 4–5 minutes, basting as necessary. When the fish is cooked it should flake easily.

Turbot Salad

The fish can be cooked in advance and left to cool.

900 g (2 lb) turbot or any other white fish	100 g (4 oz) button mushrooms
600 ml (1 pt) water	225 g (8 oz) frozen prawns, thawed
150 ml (¼ pt) milk	3 tbsp parsley
2 lemons	salt and cayenne pepper
10 tbsp olive oil	freshly ground black pepper
1 small onion	lettuce or Chinese leaves

1 Wash the fish and poach it in the water and milk with a little salt and a few parsley stalks for about 15 minutes, until it is firm. Drain the fish, discarding the liquor (or you can use it for a fish soup or fish stock). Remove the skin and bones. If the fish is to be left for some time, allow it to cool, then store it in the refrigerator in a covered container.
2 To assemble the salad, flake the fish into large pieces.
3 Squeeze the juice from both lemons and grate the rind from one.
4 Pour the olive oil into a bowl and whisk in the lemon juice and rind.
5 Peel and finely chop the onion. Trim and thinly slice the mushrooms.
6 Carefully stir the onion, mushrooms, prawns and most of the parsley into the oil, season with salt, pepper and a pinch of cayenne pepper, and lastly stir in the flaked fish.
7 Serve on a bed of washed lettuce or Chinese leaves, garnished with a sprinkling of the reserved parsley.

Sesame Beef

All the work—all 5 minutes of it—is done the night before or in the morning. The beef is already in a sauce and simply has to be heated.

675 g (1½ lb) sirloin of beef	*1 tbsp sesame seeds*
1 medium-sized onion	*1 tsp tomato purée*
1 large clove garlic	*1 tbsp flour*
2 tbsp olive oil	*salt*
6 tbsp soy sauce	*175 g (6 oz) button mushrooms*
4 tbsp soft dark brown sugar	*150 ml (¼ pt) water*
1 tbsp red pepper sauce	

1 Trim the beef and cut it into very thin strips.
2 Peel and thinly slice the onion. Peel and crush the garlic.
3 In a large bowl, beat together the olive oil, soy sauce, sugar, pepper sauce, sesame seeds, tomato purée and flour. Stir in the beef, onion and garlic, season with salt, cover and leave in a cool place until it is needed. If you prefer, transfer the contents to a polythene bag and tie securely.
4 Trim and slice the mushrooms.
5 Turn the meat and the marinade into a large pan, add the

mushrooms and water and bring to the boil, stirring. Cover the pan and simmer for 15–20 minutes, until the meat is tender. Taste for seasoning and adjust if necessary.

Orchard Beef

900 g (2 lb) rump steak, cubed *salt*
300 ml (½pt) dry cider *freshly ground black pepper*
4 tbsp white wine vinegar *12 prunes*
1 tbsp cooking oil *2 cooking apples*
1 onion, sliced

1   Put the steak, cider, wine vinegar, oil, onion, salt and pepper into a casserole, preferably flameproof, and stir to mix well. Leave in the refrigerator all day or overnight.
2   Add the prunes. Peel, core and slice the apples and add these to the casserole. If this is not flameproof, transfer the contents to a saucepan. Bring to the boil over a moderate heat, then lower the heat, cover, and simmer for 40 minutes. Check the seasoning and adjust if necessary.

Viennese Steak

900 g (2 lb) rump steak, cubed *1 tsp dried thyme*
2 medium-sized onions, chopped *3 tbsp vegetable oil*
600 ml (1 pt) medium dry cider *salt*
2 tbsp cider vinegar *freshly ground black pepper*
2 bay leaves *2 tbsp cornflour*
a pinch of powdered clove *150 ml (5 fl oz) soured cream*

1   Put the steak cubes into a polythene bag with the other ingredients except the cornflour and soured cream. Tie the top and put it on a plate in the refrigerator all day or overnight.
2   Remove the bay leaves and tip the steak and marinade into a saucepan. Bring it to the boil over moderate heat, cover, and simmer for 40 minutes. Taste and add a little more seasoning, or a pinch of sugar if you like. Blend the cornflour with a little water, stir into the saucepan and bring to the boil, stirring. Simmer for 3 minutes.
3   Remove the pan from the heat and stir in the soured cream. Gently reheat without boiling.

Spiced Pork

1 kg (2¼lb) pork fillet, thinly sliced	1 tbsp clear honey
2 cloves of garlic, crushed	1 tbsp tomato purée
1-cm (½in) root ginger, peeled and	150 ml (¼pt) dry sherry
crushed	juice of 1 lemon
1 tsp dried rosemary	1 tbsp vegetable oil
1 tsp allspice	thinly pared peel of 1 orange
salt	225 g (8 oz) sliced mushrooms
freshly ground black pepper	

1   Put all the ingredients except the mushrooms into a casserole, preferably flameproof, cover and leave in the refrigerator all day or overnight.
2   Remove the twists of orange peel, and the ginger.
3   Add the mushrooms. Bring the sauce to the boil over moderate heat, in the casserole or a saucepan, lower the heat and simmer, covered, for 30 minutes, until the meat is tender. Stir occasionally and add a little more sherry, or a little stock, if the sauce dries out.
4   Decorate with slices of fresh orange.

Pork and Prune Kebabs

A simply delicious combination.

900 g (2 lb) fillet of pork	2 tbsp red wine vinegar
24 prunes	salt
1 orange	freshly ground black pepper
4 tbsp olive oil	

1   In advance, put the prunes to soak in water.
2   Trim the pork and cut it into 2·5-cm (1-in) cubes.
3   Squeeze the juice of the orange and pare a thin strip of peel.
4   In a shallow dish or polythene bag, mix together the strained orange juice, orange rind, olive oil and wine vinegar and season with salt and pepper.
5   Turn the pork into the marinade, cover and leave in the refrigerator all day or overnight, as convenient. (If using a polythene bag, make sure it is securely tied.)
6   Drain the pork cubes from the marinade. Stone the prunes. Divide the pork and prunes equally between 6 skewers.
7   Grill them under a low heat for 15–20 minutes, brushing with the remaining marinade.

Spicy Barbecued Lamb

6 chump chops of lamb, or 12 small lamb cutlets

For the marinade
1 medium-sized onion
1 tsp dried rosemary
150 ml (¼ pt) dry cider

3 tbsp vegetable oil
3 tbsp Worcestershire sauce
2 tbsp cider vinegar
1 tbsp soft dark brown sugar
salt
freshly ground black pepper
1 lemon cut into 6 wedges

1 Peel and finely chop the onion. Put it in a small pan with all the other marinade ingredients and bring to the boil. Simmer for 3–4 minutes, then remove the pan from the heat and leave to cool.
2 Arrange the meat in a shallow dish or put it in a polythene bag, pour on the marinade, cover and leave all day, or overnight. Turn the meat at least once if possible—easy to do in a securely-tied polythene bag.
3 When you are ready to cook the lamb, remove it from the marinade with a draining spoon. Grill the chops for about 15 minutes, until they are cooked but still moist.
4 Heat the remaining marinade and serve it in a heated sauceboat.
5 Transfer the lamb to a heated serving dish and garnish it with lemon wedges.

Lamb in a Jacket

You can prepare this in advance up to stage 6.

6 lamb chops
3 eggs
1 large clove garlic
75 g (3 oz) fresh breadcrumbs
½ tsp dried rosemary

salt
freshly ground black pepper
50 g (2 oz) butter
6 large mushrooms

1 Hard-boil the eggs. Shell them and chop them finely.
2 Peel and crush the garlic.
3 Mix together the chopped egg, garlic, breadcrumbs and crushed rosemary. Season with salt and pepper.
4 Melt the butter and pour it on to the egg mixture. Stir well to make a thick paste. Allow to cool.
5 Coat each chop in the egg paste and wrap them loosely in foil. Double-seal the foil all round.

6   Place the foil parcels on a baking sheet and bake them at 220 °C (425 °F), Gas 7, for 25–30 minutes, depending on the thickness of the meat.
7   Meanwhile peel and trim the mushrooms and fry them in a little extra butter.
8   Serve each parcel opened at the top, with a mushroom garnishing the lamb.

Lamb Chops with Horseradish Cream

You can marinate the chops for several hours, then simply turn on the heat when you're ready to cook them.

6 lamb chops
1 medium-sized onion
1 large clove garlic
½ tsp dried rosemary
150 ml (¼ pt) dry cider
1 tbsp vegetable oil
1 tbsp cider vinegar
salt

freshly ground black pepper

For the sauce
6 tbsp double cream
1 tbsp cider vinegar
2 tsp grated horseradish, or 3 tsp horseradish cream

1   Peel and slice the onion. Peel and crush the garlic.
2   Arrange the chops in a flameproof casserole, scatter on the onions and garlic and crumble in the rosemary. Pour over the cider, oil and cider vinegar and season with salt and pepper.
3   Bring the liquor to the boil, cover and simmer for 20–25 minutes, until the meat is cooked.
4   Meanwhile, make the sauce. Beat the cream with the vinegar and horseradish and season it with salt and pepper.
5   When the chops are cooked, transfer them with a draining spoon to a heated serving dish and spoon the cold cream sauce over them.

Lemon Lamb Chops

6 chump-end lamb chops
1 clove garlic
4 tbsp olive oil
1 tbsp red wine vinegar
1 tbsp lemon juice

2 tsp dried rosemary
salt
freshly ground black pepper
1 lemon

1   Peel and crush the garlic and put it into a polythene bag with all the other ingredients, except the lemon. Fasten the bag securely and leave the meat to marinate for about 2 hours.

2   Line the grill pan with foil, arrange the chops and pour on the marinade. Grill under a high heat for 2 minutes on each side, baste with the sauce and lower the heat. Grill for a further 8 minutes on each side, basting occasionally.

3   Transfer the chops to a heated serving dish and pour on the remaining sauce. Garnish with wedges of lemon.

Lamb Kebabs with Mint Chutney

Store-cupboard sauces and pickles add piquancy to grilled lamb kebabs.

900 g (2 lb) lean lamb (leg)
2 pieces stem ginger
1 small carton yoghurt
4 tsp curry paste
1 tbsp white wine vinegar
2 tbsp lemon juice
1 bay leaf, crumbled

For the mint chutney
1 medium-sized onion
4 tbsp prepared mint sauce
2 tsp chilli sauce
1 tsp salt

To garnish (optional)
*1 large onion; 2 green peppers; 1
    large lemon*

1   Trim the lamb and cut it into 3·5-cm (1½-in) cubes.

2   Slice the stem ginger, mix together all the remaining marinade ingredients and stir in the lamb. Cover and leave the meat to marinate for several hours, turning it at least once if possible—a single operation if the meat has been transferred to a securely-tied polythene bag.

3   Thread the lamb on 6 skewers and grill the kebabs for 15 minutes, turning once, until cooked but still slightly pink inside.

4   Meanwhile, make the 'instant' chutney. Peel and finely chop the onion and put it in a bowl with the mint sauce, chilli sauce and salt. Stir well and serve separately.

5   If you have time to make side dishes, peel and cut the large onion into rings. Trim and cut the green pepper into rings. Cut the lemon into wedges.

6   Serve the kebabs on a bed of boiled rice, garnished with the lemon. Popadums or naan bread are good accompaniments.

Mainly from Store

Scampi Provençale

Frozen scampi, needing no preparation at all, are a marvellous stand-by for instant supper dishes, so if you like them as much as I do keep them on hand in your freezer or freezing compartment.

675 g (1½ lb) scampi, thawed
2 tbsp olive oil
1 medium-sized onion
2 cloves garlic
400-g (15-oz) can tomatoes
2 tbsp dry sherry

salt
freshly ground black pepper
1 tsp caster sugar
a pinch of mixed dried herbs
1 tbsp chopped parsley

1 Heat the oil in a saucepan.
2 Peel and chop the onion. Peel and crush the garlic. Fry them in the oil over moderate heat for about 4 minutes until the onion is soft and transparent.
3 Toss in the thawed scampi, stir carefully and fry for a couple of minutes until they become firm.
4 Tip in the tomatoes and sherry and season with salt, pepper, the sugar and dried herbs. Bring the sauce slowly to the boil, cover the pan and simmer for 5 minutes. Remove the lid and turn up the heat a little to thicken the sauce if necessary.
5 Stir in the parsley, check seasoning, and transfer to a heated serving dish.

Curried Scampi

Make the sauce overnight if it is more convenient, but it's quick enough to be made on the spot, too.

675 g (1½ lb) scampi, thawed
2 medium-sized onions
1 tbsp cooking oil

1 heaped tsp curry powder
1 tbsp flour
250 ml (scant ½ pt) water

1 tbsp tomato purée
1 tbsp desiccated coconut
1 tbsp mango, apricot or peach
    chutney

1 tbsp lemon juice
40 g (1½ oz) butter
2 tbsp sultanas
3 tbsp natural yoghurt

1   To make the sauce (which can be prepared in advance) peel and slice one of the onions. Heat the oil in a pan and fry the onion over a moderate heat for 5 minutes, until it is translucent but not beginning to colour.
2   Add the curry powder, stir, and cook for a minute or two before adding the flour. Stir well to blend.
3   Gradually pour in the water, stirring, and bring to the boil.
4   Add the tomato purée, coconut, chutney and lemon juice. Simmer the sauce for 5 minutes.
5   If you are to leave the sauce overnight, cover it closely with a circle of foil to prevent it from drying out. Strain the sauce before using it.
6   When you are ready to cook the fish, heat the butter in a saucepan or flameproof dish.
7   Peel and chop the second onion and cook it for 5 minutes.
8   Add the drained scampi and the sultanas and sauté gently for 4–5 minutes until the scampi are firm.
9   Add the strained sauce to the fish in the pan and gently stir in the yoghurt.

Andalusian Eggs (SERVES 4)

A light lunch or supper dish.

8 eggs
100 g (4 oz) ham (may be canned)
1 large onion
1 green pepper
1 small clove garlic
4 tbsp vegetable oil

325-g (12-oz) can tomatoes
225 g (8 oz) garlic sausage
150 ml (¼ pt) chicken stock, or use
    stock cube
salt
freshly ground black pepper

1   Cut the ham into strips. Peel and slice the onion. Trim the green pepper, discarding the seeds. Slice the flesh. Peel and crush the garlic.
2   Heat the oil in a saucepan and sauté the ham, onion, green pepper and garlic over a moderate heat for 3–4 minutes.
3   Drain the tomatoes and add them to the pan. Chop the sausage

into small dice and add it with the stock. Season well, bring to the boil and simmer until the mixture starts to thicken.

4   Turn the mixture into a shallow ovenproof dish, push 8 hollows with the back of a tablespoon and break in the eggs. Cover the dish with foil and bake at 190°C (375°F), Gas 5, for 8–10 minutes, until the eggs are set.

Noodles with Egg and Herring Sauce (SERVES 4)

225 g (8 oz) spaghetti or other   *salt*
   pasta   *freshly ground black pepper*
100-g (4-oz) can herring fillets   *a pinch of cayenne pepper*
150 ml (5 fl oz) soured cream   *65 g (2½ oz) butter*
1 tbsp tomato purée   *1 tsp chopped parsley garnish*
4 eggs

1   Cook the spaghetti in plenty of boiling, salted water until it is just tender—follow the directions on the packet. Refresh the cooked spaghetti quickly in cold running water, drain it again and turn it into a heated serving dish. Toss in half the butter, cover and keep warm.
2   Mix the soured cream and tomato purée together in a bowl. Drain the fish and flake it into this mixture.
3   Beat the eggs and season well with salt, pepper and a pinch of cayenne pepper.
4   Heat the remaining butter in a small saucepan, pour in the eggs and, using a wooden spoon, stir over a low heat until they start to thicken. Remove from the heat.
5   Stir the fish mixture into the eggs and allow just to heat through—the eggs mustn't harden.
6   Pour the scrambled eggs over the spaghetti and garnish with chopped parsley.

Sweet Tomato Fish

This can be served as a substantial sauce for pasta or rice, or simply with crusty French bread.

2 large onions   *1 tsp dried oregano*
1 clove garlic   *40 g (1½ oz) sultanas*
75 g (3 oz) butter   *salt*
400-g (15-oz) can tomatoes   *freshly ground black pepper*
2 198-g (7-oz) cans tuna fish   *a pinch of cayenne pepper*

Photograph: Bacofoil Ltd

6. Plaice with Roman Sauce (page 73). Whole fish or fillets, butter-glazed fresh or frozen vegetables cook to perfection in envelopes of foil.

Photograph: British Bacon Bureau

7. Bacon Ratatouille (page 85). A medley of tender summer vegetables with crispy cubes of bacon.

Photograph: (Fred Mancini) courtesy British Meat (top) and Jif Lemon (bottom)

8. Spiced Lamb Chops (top, page 89) and St. Clement's Chicken (bottom, page 98) prove that fruit and meat are perfect partners.

Photograph: (Fred Mancini) courtesy Gale's Honey

9. Chocolate Rum Cake (page 159), Atholl Brose (page 145) and Caramel Pears (page 151) make a tempting trio.

1   Peel and slice the onions. Peel and crush the garlic.
2   Gently fry the onions and garlic in the butter for 5 minutes,
    tip in the tomatoes. Stir well and carefully stir in the drain
    tuna fish, oregano, sultanas and the seasoning. Bring gradual
    to the boil, lower the heat and simmer for 10 minutes. Remove
    from the heat and turn into a heated serving dish.

Noodles with Herbed Tomato Sauce

2 tbsp vegetable oil	*freshly ground black pepper*
1 large onion	*450 g (1 lb) thin noodles*
400-g (15-oz) can tomatoes	*40 g (1½ oz) butter*
3 tbsp tomato purée	*175 g (6 oz) Gruyère cheese*
1 tsp dried oregano	*75 g (3 oz) Parmesan cheese*
salt	*1 tbsp fresh chopped parsley*

1   Heat the oil in a pan. Peel and finely chop the onion and
    fry it over moderate heat for 5–6 minutes, stirring once or twice.
2   Tip in the can of tomatoes, add the tomato purée, oregano, salt
    and pepper. Stir and bring to the boil, then lower the heat,
    cover the pan and simmer for 20 minutes.
3   Meanwhile, cook the noodles in plenty of boiling, salted water
    in a large uncovered pan. (Follow the directions on the packet
    for the exact cooking time.) Drain the noodles into a colander,
    run cold water through them and drain them well. Gently
    reheat the noodles in the pan with the butter.
4   Dice the Gruyère cheese.
5   Tip the tomato sauce on to the noodles and stir in the cheeses.
    Toss over a low heat until the cheese has melted.
6   Turn into a heated serving dish and garnish with the parsley.
    Crusty French bread goes well with this simple pasta dish.

Quick Lasagne

225 g (8 oz) oven-ready lasagne	*salt*
1 large onion	*freshly ground black pepper*
1 clove garlic	*150 ml (¼ pt) chicken stock, or use*
2 tbsp vegetable oil	* stock cube*
450-g (1-lb) can best minced beef	*225 g (8 oz) cottage cheese*
400-g (15-oz) can peeled tomatoes	*1 small carton yoghurt*
2 tbsp tomato purée	*50 g (2 oz) Parmesan cheese*
1 tsp dried oregano	

1   Peel and slice the onion. Peel and crush the garlic.
2   Heat the oil in a pan. Fry the onion and garlic for 5 minutes over
    moderate heat. Tip in the cans of minced beef and tomatoes,
    add the tomato purée, season with the herb, plenty of salt and
    pepper and pour on the stock. Stir well and leave to simmer
    uncovered for 10 minutes.
3   Beat the cottage cheese, yoghurt and grated Parmesan cheese
    together.
4   In the greased ovenproof dish, spread layers of the meat mix-
    ture, lasagne and cheese sauce, finishing with cheese sauce.
    You can assemble the dish to this stage in advance.
5   Bake at 190 °C (375 °F), Gas 5, for 45 minutes, until the sauce is
    brown and bubbling.

Baked Pasta

The casserole can be cooking while you are eating the first course.

450 g (1 lb) pasta shapes (e.g.   *2 275-g (10-oz) cans condensed*
    wagon wheels)   *tomato soup*
50 g (2 oz) butter   *198-g (7-oz) can tuna fish*
2 medium-sized onions   *1 tsp dried oregano*
1 clove garlic   *225 g (8 oz) Parmesan cheese*
225 g (8 oz) mushrooms   *salt*
                                           freshly ground black pepper

1   Cook the pasta in an uncovered pan in plenty of boiling,
    salted water, following the directions on the packet. Drain
    it into a colander, run cold water through it and drain well
    again.
2   Peel and slice the onions. Peel and crush the garlic. Wipe and
    slice the mushrooms.
3   Melt the butter in a large pan and gently fry the onions and
    garlic for 5 minutes, then add the mushrooms and fry for a
    further 3 minutes, stirring occasionally.
4   Tip in the tomato soup, stir in the drained and flaked fish, dried
    herb, three-quarters of the grated cheese and the salt and
    pepper. Add the cooked pasta, stir well and pour into a
    large greased baking dish. Sprinkle the remaining cheese on
    top.
5   Bake in the oven at 180 °C (350 °F), Gas 4, for 40 minutes until

the cheese is golden brown. French bread is a good accompaniment.

Eggs Baked in Soured Cream

12 *small eggs*
300 *ml* (½*pt*) *soured cream*
2 *tbsp chopped chives*
2 *tbsp chopped parsley*
salt

freshly ground black pepper
4 *tbsp breadcrumbs*
75 *g* (3 *oz*) *cheese*
40 *g* (1½*oz*) *butter*

1 Mix together the soured cream, half the chives and half the parsley and season with salt and pepper. Pour the mixture into a large, shallow ovenproof dish.
2 Break the eggs into the dish and season them lightly.
3 Put the breadcrumbs into a bowl, stir in the remaining chives and parsley and grate the cheese into it. Season with salt and pepper and sprinkle over the eggs.
4 Melt the butter and pour it over the crumb topping.
5 Bake at 190 °C (375 °F), Gas 5, for 8 minutes until the eggs are just set and the topping is golden brown.

Bacon and Egg Pancake (SERVES 3)

The kind of dish you could serve when it's so late it's almost breakfast-time!

6 *bacon rashers*
4 *large eggs*
1 *tbsp flour*
6 *tbsp milk*
salt

freshly ground black pepper
¼ *tsp mixed dried herbs*
15 *g* (½*oz*) *butter*
3 *tomatoes to garnish*

1 Cut the rind from the bacon rashers and grill them until they are crisp.
2 Beat together the eggs, flour and milk—a blender makes quick work of it—and season well with salt, pepper and the dried herbs.
3 Heat the butter in a frying-pan until it is just turning brown. Pour in the egg mixture and cook over a fairly high heat until just set—lift the edges occasionally with a spatula.
4 Arrange the bacon rashers, wheel-like, on top and garnish with fresh tomato slices.

Pipérade

This could also be served as a first course.

8 eggs	*795-g (1 lb 12-oz) can tomatoes*
6 green peppers	*a large pinch of dried basil*
1 medium-sized onion	*salt*
1 large clove garlic	*freshly ground black pepper*
2 tbsp olive oil	

1   Beat the eggs thoroughly in a bowl.
2   Trim the green peppers, discarding the seeds, and cut them into chunks. Peel and slice the onion. Peel and finely chop the garlic.
3   Heat the oil in a large, heavy frying-pan and fry the onion and garlic over a moderate heat until the onion just starts to turn yellow. Add the peppers and cook, stirring occasionally, for 12–15 minutes. The peppers should be still firm and not broken up.
4   Tip in the can of tomatoes, add the basil, salt and pepper and stir well. Break up the tomatoes with a wooden spoon. Cook until the mixture thickens.
5   Add the beaten eggs and stir until they begin to thicken. Remove the pan from the heat just before the scrambled eggs set—they should still be moist.
6   Tip the pipérade out on to a large heated plate and serve with hot French bread.

To make the dish more substantial, you can serve grilled bacon rashers.

Asparagus Soufflé (SERVES 3)

You wouldn't normally decide to serve a soufflé in a fast-food situation. But this one's cheating. The quantity given serves three. It's best to make two separate ones for six people—it works better than the double quantity.

298-g (10½-oz) can condensed	*salt*
* asparagus soup*	*freshly ground black pepper*
250-g (8¾-oz) can asparagus tips	*drops of hot red pepper sauce*
5 eggs	

1   Tip the condensed soup into a blender. Drain the asparagus tips and, reserving a few to garnish, put the rest in the blender. Whizz until smooth.

2 Pour the asparagus mixture into a saucepan and heat.
3 Separate the eggs. Use an electric beater to beat the yolks until they are thick and creamy. Add them to the hot (but not boiling) soup and cook, stirring, for 3 minutes. Do not allow to boil. Take the pan from the heat and season well.
4 Whisk the egg whites and fold them into the asparagus mixture.
5 Pour into an oiled 900-ml (1½-pt) soufflé dish and bake at 190°C (375°F), Gas 5, for 35–40 minutes, until the soufflé is well risen and golden brown. Decorate with the reserved asparagus tips and serve at once.

Salad Niçoise

A salad that is a light but substantial supper dish with the help of a few store-cupboard cans.

4 eggs
450-g (16-oz) can green beans
198-g (7-oz) can tuna fish
50-g (1¾-oz) can anchovy fillets
2 peppers, 1 green, 1 red

3 tomatoes
12 black olives
1 lettuce or Chinese leaves
French dressing

1 Hard-boil the eggs. Shell and then quarter them.
2 Drain the can of green beans, the tuna fish and the anchovy fillets.
3 Trim the green and the red peppers, discarding the seeds, and slice them. Quarter the tomatoes.
4 Mix together the beans, flaked tuna fish, anchovy fillets, pepper strips, tomatoes, olives and eggs.
5 Wash and dry the lettuce and line a large salad bowl with it. Pile the salad ingredients in. Just before serving, pour over French dressing.

6

ACCOMPANIMENTS

Speedy dishes are not the all-in-together, vegetables and meat in one pot kind, and usually need something to add bulk, take up the sauce, or provide texture variety.

Apart from good, wholesome bread, rice and pasta are the fastest 'company' food of all, since they need no preparation and little attention during cooking. Vegetables and salads do need a certain amount of preparation, even if it is only washing and slicing. Some are speedier than others, and I have selected the ones I personally find quickest and easiest.

Rice

Rice is the perfect fast cooking accompaniment. It needs no prep-arations, and cooks in about a quarter of an hour—but, to be honest, it isn't entirely accident-proof.

There's a new and much improved version of that well-known quick-cook rice, Uncle Ben's. If you already know the product, but haven't tried it for some time, it is well worth giving it another chance. If you follow the instructions on the packet absolutely to the letter, you will find that your rice is not only fluffy and well separated, but has a delicious nutty, crunchy texture.

However, I have recently tried something else new, and have been—almost—completely converted. This is boil-in-the-bag rice, a good quality long-grain rice in a form which, as far as I can tell from a dozen or so testings, is really disaster-proof. For 4–6 serv-ings, you boil about 2 litres (3 pints) of salted water, drop in two or three perforated bags of the rice—each one contains 100 g (4 oz)—bring the water back to the boil and simmer for 15 minutes. Lift out the bags and tip the rice into a heated, buttered serving dish. The rice absorbs the cooking liquid through the perforations in the bags, so you can perfectly well use stock instead of water, and there's no need to strain it at the end. I don't think cooking can be made much simpler than that.

Just for revision, here are the two main methods of cooking long-grain rice, both of which, if carefully followed, can produce perfect results each time. The first, the rapid boiling method, relies on the use of a very large saucepan and plenty of water, which must be boiling before the rice is added, and brought quickly to the boil after. In the second, the simmering method, the rice absorbs all the cooking liquid and dries in the pan, without straining. Success here depends on having the right proportion of liquid to rice, so both must be measured.

Rapid Boiling Method

Allow 40–50 g (1½–2 oz) long-grain rice for each serving.

325 g (12 oz) long-grain rice *1 tbsp lemon juice (optional)*
about 3·5 litres (6 pts) water *1 tbsp vegetable oil (optional)*
3 tsp salt *butter (see method)*

1 Tip the rice into a sieve and wash it in cold water. Pick out any discoloured grains and drain the rice thoroughly.
2 Bring the salted water to the boil in a very large saucepan. The addition of lemon juice helps to preserve the whiteness of the rice. A little vegetable oil helps to 'settle' the boiling water and prevent it from boiling over—literally pouring oil on troubled waters!
3 When the water is boiling, tip in the drained rice and stir it thoroughly with a wooden spoon to break up any lumps that have formed. Cover the pan and bring the water back to the boil quickly. Lower the heat and simmer for 10–15 minutes, until the rice is just tender but not soft—*al dente*, as it is called in Italy. To test the rice, take out a few grains on a spoon and break them with a fingernail. If they are still hard in the centre, continue cooking for a minute or two more before testing again. The exact cooking time varies according to the type of rice—some varieties are harder than others.
4 When the rice is cooked, tip it into a colander (reserving the cooking liquid for soup or stew) and run cold water through it. Drain the rice again, then turn it into a well-greased heated serving dish, cover and set it to dry and re-heat in a cool oven. For extra flavour, stir in a knob of butter. Garnish the rice as appropriate, with a sprinkling of chopped herbs or a little paprika pepper.

Simmered Rice—to serve 6 or more

The amount of water or stock must be accurately measured, since it is to be completely absorbed by the rice. The proportion is always 300 ml (½ pint) liquid to each 100 g (4 oz) long-grain rice.

325 g (12 oz) long-grain rice *1½ level tsp salt*
900 ml (1½ pts) water or stock *butter (see method)*

1 Wash the rice thoroughly in cold water, discarding any discoloured grains. Drain well.

2   Choose a heavy-based pan with a well-fitting lid—it can be a saucepan or a large frying-pan. Brush the base with oil or wipe it with a buttered paper to prevent the rice grains from sticking.
3   Put the rice, water or stock and salt into the pan and bring to the boil. Stir once with a wooden spoon, lower the heat and cover the pan. Simmer very gently without stirring again for 15 minutes. Do not lift the lid during this time, but now test to see if the rice is cooked—the exact time will depend on the variety of rice. If the grains are still hard in the centre, cover the pan and simmer for a few minutes more, adding a little more water or stock if necessary. In this case, lightly fluff up the rice with a fork—a wooden spoon or plastic one if the pan surface is non-stick.
4   When the rice is cooked, take the pan from the heat and leave it in a warm place, still covered, for 5–10 minutes before serving. Turn the rice into a well-buttered serving dish, and, if you like, stir in a knob of butter.

Cheese Rice

As a variation for rice to be served with grilled meat or fish, stir in 50 g (2 oz) grated hard cheese such as Parmesan, 1 teaspoon chopped fresh parsley and a good grinding of black pepper just before serving.

Adding Colour to Rice

As rice takes up not only the flavour but also the colour of the liquid in which it is cooked—rice cooked in chicken stock will be parchment-coloured, not white—adding colour is often a good way to introduce variety and eye-appeal. Vegetable dyes such as saffron and turmeric, both of which give a pleasing golden yellow, have been used for centuries, and saffron, of course, is the traditional spice of Spanish cuisine. Mix $\frac{1}{2}$ level teaspoon saffron powder with 1 tablespoon of water or stock, and stir it into the cooked rice. Turmeric, a less precious commodity, can be added with the water in the proportion of 1 rounded teaspoon for the rapid boiling method, and $\frac{1}{2}$ level teaspoon for simmering.

Other colours can be achieved by adding a few drops of natural food colouring to the cooking liquid. In this way, rice can be tinged pale shades of green, brown, orange and so on. But care should be taken to avoid the bizarre!

Saffron Pepper Rice
Good with chicken.

325 g (12 oz) long-grain rice	*2 large peppers, 1 red, 1 green*
salted water or chicken stock	*2 tbsp vegetable oil*
½ tsp saffron powder	

1 Cook the rice by your chosen method and add the saffron powder as described.
2 Meanwhile, trim the peppers and discard the seeds. Chop the flesh finely. Heat the oil in a small pan and fry the peppers over a moderate heat until they are just tender, but not beginning to brown.
3 Stir the peppers into the cooked rice and turn it into a well-buttered heated serving dish.

Quick Vegetable Rice

To add accents of colour, shape and texture to boiled rice, add a small quantity of thawed frozen vegetables just before the end of cooking time. Peas and sweetcorn kernels—100 g (4 oz) of each—make a good contrast. Add them about 5 minutes before the end of the rapid boiling method, and return the water quickly to the boil. Or stir them in about two-thirds of the way through simmering.

Pilaf

Rice for pilaf is cooked in a similar way to the 'simmering' method—the difference being that it is first tossed in hot butter or oil until the grains are shiny and transparent. It is the perfect vehicle for all kinds of additions—frozen or canned vegetables, fresh, frozen or canned fruit, dried fruits, nuts, cooked meat or fish are all suitable. The following recipe is a typical example of a Middle-Eastern pilaf, a perfect accompaniment to a plain meat dish.

Raisin and Nut Pilaf

250 g (9 oz) long-grain rice	*salt*
3 tbsp vegetable oil, or	*freshly ground black pepper*
40 g (1½ oz) butter	*125 g (5 oz) raisins*
1 small clove garlic	*65 g (2½ oz) blanched whole*
1 small onion	* almonds*
650 ml (just over 1 pt) chicken	*an extra 25 g (1 oz) butter*
* stock, or use stock cube*	

1 Wash and drain the rice.
2 Heat the oil or butter in a heavy pan that has a lid.
3 Peel and crush the garlic. Peel and finely chop the onion.
4 Fry the rice, garlic and onion in the pan until the rice grains are transparent—just a minute or so.
5 Pour on the stock, season with salt and pepper and stir. Bring to the boil, cover the pan and simmer over a low heat for 15–20 minutes, until all the stock is absorbed and the rice is just tender. Remove the pan from the heat and leave it to stand undisturbed, and still covered, for 10 minutes.
6 Stir in the raisins and almonds and the 25 g (1 oz) butter, cover and stand in a warm place or over a very low heat (preferably on an asbestos mat) for a further 5 minutes.

Orange Rice

This must be cooked by the 'simmering' method, so that the rice takes up all the spices. Very good with pork, veal and chicken, lightly spiced and sunshine gold.

325 g (12 oz) long-grain rice
1 orange
750 ml (1¼ pts) chicken stock, or
*   use stock cubes*
½ tsp powdered turmeric

¼ tsp ground coriander
¼ tsp ground ginger
salt
freshly ground black pepper
25 g (1 oz) butter

1 Wash and drain the rice.
2 Squeeze and strain the juice and grate the rind of the orange.
3 Choose a pan with a well-fitting lid. Put the rice, grated orange rind and chicken stock in the pan. Stir in the spices, salt and pepper, bring to the boil, then cover the pan and simmer over a low heat for about 15 minutes, without lifting the lid or stirring.
4 Test to see if the rice is cooked. When it is, stir in the orange juice and the butter. Leave the rice to rest in the covered pan for 5 minutes before tipping it into a heated serving dish.

Spanish Rice

Moistened and almost sauce-like because of the high proportion of tomatoes, this savoury rice is good with 'dry' dishes, particularly grilled or fried meat or grilled fish.

250 g (9 oz) long-grain rice
1 medium-sized onion

1 clove garlic
1 green pepper

2 tbsp olive oil
425-g (15-oz) can tomatoes
2 tsp sugar
salt

freshly ground black pepper
1 bay leaf
½ tsp dried oregano
50 g (2 oz) Parmesan cheese

1 Wash and drain the rice and cook it by your preferred method.
2 Meanwhile, peel and chop the onion. Peel and crush the garlic. Trim the green pepper, discarding the seeds, and chop the flesh.
3 Heat the oil in a large saucepan and fry the prepared vegetables over a moderate heat for 4–5 minutes.
4 Tip in the can of tomatoes, add the sugar, salt, black pepper, bay leaf and dried herb and bring to the boil. Cover the pan and simmer for 15 minutes.
5 Turn the cooked rice into the saucepan and stir well, then transfer to a well-buttered serving dish. It will wait happily in a low oven and is then sprinkled with grated Parmesan just before serving.

Banana Fried Rice

A good accompaniment to chicken or curry dishes.

275 g (10 oz) long-grain rice
water or stock for cooking
1 medium-sized onion
50 g (2 oz) butter, or 4 tbsp
  vegetable oil

4 bananas
salt
1 rounded tsp curry powder
1 lemon

1 Wash the rice and cook it by your preferred method.
2 While the rice is cooking, peel and chop the onion.
3 Heat the butter or oil in a frying-pan. Peel and thickly slice the bananas, lightly fry them for a minute or two and remove them with a draining spoon. Keep them warm.
4 Fry the onion in the pan for 4–5 minutes over a moderate heat until it is tender and just turning golden brown.
5 When the rice is cooked and, if necessary, strained, tip it into the pan, add salt and the curry powder and stir-fry it until the rice is glistening and hot. Carefully stir in the banana slices, and turn it into a heated, buttered serving dish. Garnish the rice with a light sprinkling of curry powder. Serve with lemon wedges.

Pasta

Pasta of all kinds, like rice, simply cooked and tossed in butter makes an ideal accompaniment to most main dishes, but particularly those with ample sauces. There's immense variety—long spaghetti, short-cut macaroni, broad and baby noodles, green noodles, folded ones called tagliatelli, shells, wheels, stars, and many more—it stores almost indefinitely in an airtight container and needs absolutely no preparation.

Cooking Pasta

As a main-dish accompaniment, allow about 50 g (2 oz) dry pasta per person—that's a generous helping, though the Italians man-·age considerably more. Allow 1·75 litres (3 pints) water and ½ tablespoon oil. Sprinkle the pasta gradually into the boiling water. Guide long spaghetti so that it curls round inside the pan. Stir it once with a wooden spoon or fork to stop it sticking and bring it back as quickly as possible to the boil. *Do not cover the pan at any stage.* Lower the heat and simmer gently for the time directed on the packet—this varies according to the type of pasta, the size and the shape. Squidged-up pasta can mean one of these things: not enough water was used in the first place; the water was not brought back to the boil quickly enough or the pasta was cooked for too long.

As a general guide, long spaghetti is cooked in 10 minutes and short-cut macaroni in 8 minutes, smaller shapes in less time—a factor in their favour. Test the pasta as soon as you think it should be ready, to be sure not to overcook it. It should be only just tender.

If you can find 'home-made' pasta in a delicatessen, you can cut a little off the cooking time. Because it has not been dried, it cooks more quickly—in 5–7 minutes. Allow about twice as much fresh pasta per serving.

Look out, too, for branded makes of 'quick-cooking' pasta,

which take from 2 minutes for egg noodles to 7 minutes for long macaroni.

When the pasta is cooked, drain it into a large colander. Some cooks—I am one—run cold water through it to refresh it and help to separate the strands, then gently heat it with a little butter in a pan. Otherwise, turn the drained pasta into a well-greased heated serving dish and stir in a knob of butter or a tablespoon of olive oil, to glisten the surface and prevent sticking.

Vegetable Pasta

Ring the changes by adding thawed frozen vegetables to the pasta part-way through the cooking time, or cooked vegetables at the end, just to be warmed through. Peas, cut green beans, sweetcorn kernels, cooked or canned kidney beans, pineapple chunks, all make interesting additions.

Pasta Salads

Any leftover cooked pasta can be served cold as a salad. Indeed, pasta salads are so good that they are well worth planning as unusual accompaniments to the main dish. Cook the pasta the night before. Mix it while it is still hot with a vinaigrette dressing, or any of the flavoured variations (pages 178–80). Or cool the pasta and mix it with mayonnaise, or flavoured mayonnaise (pages 173–5). Store the dressed pasta in a covered container in the refrigerator—and that's one job out of the way.

Maryland Salad

175 g (6 oz) short-cut pasta (mini   *200 ml (good ¼ pt) mayonnaise*
  shells or rings)   *salt*
2 canned red pimentos   *freshly ground black pepper*
175 g (6 oz) whole sweetcorn   *1 tbsp chopped parsley*
  kernels

1   Cook the pasta perhaps the night before, and when it is ready drain it in a colander.
2   Meanwhile, chop the canned pimento, discarding the seeds.
3   Drain the canned sweetcorn into a bowl, stir in the pimento, mayonnaise, salt, pepper and parsley. Stir in the drained pasta and either serve straight away or store in a covered container in the refrigerator.

Spiced Pasta Salad

This salad goes well with grilled fish or chicken.

175 g (6 oz) pasta shells
3 stalks celery
2 canned pimentos
2 275-g (10-oz) jars prawn
   cocktail sauce

salt
freshly ground black pepper
a pinch of cayenne pepper

1   Cook the pasta. Test, and when it is ready drain it in a colander
    and refresh in cold water. Drain again, shaking the colander
    well—water collects inside the shells.
2   While the pasta is cooking, wash and finely chop or cut the
    celery. Chop the canned pimento, discarding the seeds.
3   Mix all the ingredients together and, if not serving straight
    away, store in the refrigerator in a covered container.

Mango Pasta Salad

Good with grilled steak or chicken.

175 g (6 oz) short-cut pasta
   (macaroni or wagon wheels)
2 green peppers
4 tbsp mango chutney sauce

1 tsp curry powder
300 ml (½ pt) mayonnaise
1 tbsp lemon juice

1   Cook the pasta. When it is ready, drain it, run cold water
    through it and drain it again. This refreshing in cold water,
    apart from separating the pasta shapes, speeds up the cooling.
2   Meanwhile, trim the green peppers, discarding the seeds, and
    chop the flesh.
3   Mix all the ingredients together in a bowl. Store if necessary in a
    covered container in the refrigerator.

Vegetables

Whenever I serve fresh vegetables I take care to choose those that need the very minimum of preparation. Whooshing them under the tap in a great hurry, I'd never be entirely happy that I had grubbed the last grain of sand nestling in the very heart of leeks. And much as I used to love, as a child, sitting in the garden shelling peas, times have changed. In those days, I wasn't expecting five people to descend on me off the next train.

I usually cook vegetables by one of four methods: baking or boiling in foil (page 132); simmering in equal quantities of well-seasoned stock and butter—about 6 tablespoons of stock to 50 g (2 oz) butter for 6 servings; steaming (page 133), or Chinese stir-frying (page 133).

Green Beans

Choose tender young ones that just need snipping at each end or, at the most, breaking in half. Steam young ones whole with a spoonful of chopped spring onion and a good grinding of pepper and salt for 15–20 minutes. Toss in plenty of butter to glaze them. Or stir-fry.

Broccoli

It needs a good head of cold water from the tap, a quick trim and it's ready for steaming. Serve with blender hollandaise sauce (page 175) or a crunchy garnish (page 184). Or stir-fry.

Brussels Sprouts

Choose tight, fat little ones and you don't have to cut those tedious crosses in the base. Steam them and garnish with chopped walnuts, or toss them in soured cream. Or stir-fry. To boil them, use a minimum of water and leave the pan uncovered for the first 15 minutes. This stops them yellowing.

Carrots

Young ones rarely need more than scrubbing with a vegetable brush or scraping with a knife. And large ones can be pushed very speedily through a potato chipper, to come out in quickie-cook strips. Blanch whole ones before simmering in stock and butter. Glaze with more butter and garnish with dried mint stirred into caster sugar. Or slice very thinly and stir-fry.

Cauliflower

Quick to wash and just as quick to break into tiny florets—which cuts down on cooking time. Steam, or simmer florets in stock and butter for 10–12 minutes. They like a crunchy cheesy or garlic topping (page 184). Or stir-fry.

Chicory

It only needs trimming at the base and, because it is so good and firm, is quick and reassuring to wash. Boil the whole heads in very little salted water or stock, barely enough to cover, with 50 g (2 oz) butter and a good few grindings of pepper. When the vegetable is tender, 3 tablespoons of cream stirred in thickens the pan juices and makes an instant sauce.

Chinese Leaves

They are in the shops for most of the winter and simply need slicing through the whole head. Or separate the leaves and break or cut each one into large pieces. Thinly sliced, they need cooking for only 3–4 minutes in boiling, salted water or simmering in stock and butter for 10–12 minutes. They are delicious stir-fried.

Courgettes

Tiny ones, freshly in season, are one of the delights of the summer. Small ones just need trimming and even the larger ones just need chopping into fat little chunks. I usually blanch whole ones or chunks quickly in boiling salted water, drain them and dry them on kitchen paper, then stir-fry them in very hot butter with a couple of pinches of dried oregano. Garnish with buttered bread crumbs.

Fennel

My favourite of all vegetables. I cook it in exactly the same way as chicory, sometimes adding cream to thicken the vegetable stock, sometimes stirring in a knob of *beurre-manié*, flour and butter worked together, to do the same. A few crushed fennel seeds scattered on top—there couldn't be a better garnish.

Mushrooms

I never wash or peel them, just tidy up the stalk end and wipe them with damp kitchen paper. I crush a clove of garlic into about 50–75 g (2–3 oz) butter in a small pan and turn the mushrooms in it for 3–4 minutes. A couple of tablespoons of cream and plenty of seasoning added to the pan juices makes a heavenly sauce.

Mushrooms in Brandy

For special occasions—and every time you entertain friends it *is* a special occasion—here's a simple but delightful way to serve a vegetable we can buy fresh all the year round. It's specially good with veal or chicken.

450 g (1 lb) button mushrooms   *salt*
50 g (2 oz) butter   *freshly ground black pepper*
3 tbsp brandy
150 ml ($\frac{1}{4}$ pt) chicken stock, or use
  stock cube

1   Trim the mushrooms.
2   Heat the butter in a pan and sauté the mushrooms over a low heat for 3–4 minutes.
3   Add the brandy, stock and seasoning, bring to the boil, cover the pan and simmer for about 8 minutes. Lift out the mushrooms with a draining spoon and transfer them to a heated serving dish. Rapidly boil the sauce to reduce it a little, then pour it over the mushrooms.

Potatoes

Without them, unfortunately, some people really don't feel they have had a meal. Here's a good way to ring the changes on sautéd potatoes. Cook small peeled potatoes whole until they are just tender. Drain them and toss in a good knob of butter. Shake the pan until the potatoes are well coated, then toss in a handful of porridge oats. Put the pan over a low heat and shake it occasionally. Crisply fried oats make a lovely jacket!

Spinach

The meticulous washing it needs can be a complete turn-off for most cooks in a hurry. But stir-fried (for method see page 134) spinach is so good that you may think it worth trying. You can wash the spinach the night before and leave it in a large plastic bag in the refrigerator.

Cooking Vegetables in Foil

Vegetables wrapped in foil can be baked at the same time as the main dish if you are using the oven, or boiled in a pan of water on top of the cooker. Prepare the vegetables in the usual way, season them well with salt and pepper and add a knob of butter. Add 1 tablespoon of water or stock to hard vegetables such as carrots and potatoes. Make a loose parcel of the foil, with plenty of room above the vegetables, and double-seal the edges securely. You can garnish the cooked vegetables with chopped fresh herbs and another knob of butter. The following approximate cooking times are for 450 g (1 lb) of vegetables, at an oven temperature of 200 °C (400 °F), Gas 6:

Peas will be cooked in 15–20 minutes
Mushrooms (100 g ($\frac{1}{4}$ lb)) in 20 minutes
Sliced courgettes in 25 minutes
Broad beans, green beans, broccoli, cabbage (shredded), marrow
    rings, sliced green or red peppers, chopped spinach, sweetcorn
    kernels and whole tomatoes, in 30 minutes
Sliced carrots, whole corn-on-the-cob and sliced potatoes in 40
    minutes

FROZEN VEGETABLES

You can cook frozen vegetables in foil, too. Put the unfrozen block of vegetables on to a piece of foil, season with salt and pepper and add a knob of butter. Make a loose parcel, as for fresh vegetables. Bake or boil for the following times:

Frozen chopped spinach, 20 minutes
Frozen peas and broad beans, 25 minutes

Frozen sliced green beans, sweetcorn kernels and mixed vegetables, 30 minutes
Frozen Brussels sprouts, 40 minutes

Steaming Vegetables

Steaming is a good way to cook vegetables, especially green beans,
broccoli, Brussels sprouts and cauliflower, because it preserves all
the colour and 'goodness'. Most vegetables, cut into dice, florets or
chunks, steam in 15–20 minutes, and should then be served
straight away.

EQUIPMENT

You don't really need any special equipment, though you can of
course buy special steaming pans in all sizes. I have what is called a
steamer fan, a perforated metal disc surrounded by folding perforated metal flaps that open out to form a dish shape. The fan fits
tightly into any saucepan from 15 cm (6 in) upwards, then the lid
goes on top. Or you can improvise by using a small colander in a
large pan, or by putting the vegetables on a heated plate or shallow
dish on a trivet. Choose a pan with a well-fitting lid, to trap all the
available steam, and have a little water boiling in the base.

THE METHOD

Bring the water to a rapid boil, then put in the food and tightly
cover with the lid. The water in the pan must be kept at a steady
boil throughout—you do need a good head of steam.

GARNISHING

Steamed vegetables take well to a little last-minute titivation before
they are served, so have the garnish ready. Turn them first into a
good knob of butter, to give them creaminess and sparkle, then
add buttered crumbs, chopped nuts, crisply-fried bacon, mini
croûtons fried in garlic butter, chopped spring onions, herbs or a
pinch of spice. For more ideas, see Finishing Touches (page 168).

Stir-fried Vegetables

Fresh vegetables cooked the Chinese way are perfect for the fast-
food occasion. Cooked for the very minimum of time in very hot oil
and their own natural juices, they are literally given a 'flash in the
pan'; they retain all their natural colour, flavour and texture, and
look so appetizing that added garnish is unnecessary.

Practise a few times until you can stir-fry practically blindfold, without having to refer to a recipe. It takes longer to read about it than do it!

Vegetables are divided into three categories, soft, semi-hard and hard. *Soft vegetables* such as bean sprouts, lettuce, spinach, courgettes, mushrooms, tomatoes and watercress, are the ones with a high moisture content. These release their own juices on contact with the hot oil and so can be cooked without the addition of any liquid. Among the *semi-hard vegetables* are celery, cabbage, Brussels sprouts, mange-tout peas and bamboo shoots. *Hard vegetables* include broccoli, cauliflower, asparagus, carrots, runner beans, green beans and turnips. Hard and semi-hard vegetables need a very little liquid, usually stock or water, added after the initial stir-frying, then they finish cooking in the steam.

PREPARING VEGETABLES FOR STIR-FRYING

Cut into neat, even sized pieces, so that the maximum area is exposed to the heat.

According to type, the vegetables may be sliced, diced or shredded. The Chinese, masters in the art, use cleavers to cut wafer-thin slices, but we need not be ashamed to resort to slicing or shredding appliances or attachments in the interest of speed. You can do the preparation in advance, as long as the prepared vegetables are tightly wrapped in foil or cling film or put into an airtight lidded container in the refrigerator. Soft vegetables are usually sliced vertically or straight, and semi-hard and hard ones sliced diagonally. (You will find more details on how to prepare vegetables in Fast Methods, beginning on page 24.)

Some vegetables composed of two distinct textures, such as cabbage or Swiss chard, are treated as two different vegetables. Tear the soft green leaves away from the tough stalks. Stir-fry the leaves as for other soft vegetables, thinly slice the stalks and treat them as semi-hard.

COOKING PANS FOR STIR-FRYING

The Chinese use a wok, a cone-shaped pan that fits snugly over a gas ring. But you can use a good-quality heavy-based frying-pan.

THE METHOD

Thoroughly heat the pan over a high heat before adding the oil. Pour in a little vegetable oil—usually peanut oil—or lard, and allow to become sizzling hot. A little salt added to the oil makes green vegetables an even brighter green. Drop the prepared vegetables into the sizzling oil and quickly stir them with a wooden spoon so that all the surfaces are coated straight away. If the oil is not hot enough, soft vegetables will collapse. As long as this stage is carried out quickly, the vegetables will not burn. Leaf vegetables, the most vulnerable, will have just enough water drops clinging to them after washing to see them through safely until their natural moisture starts to run. Immediately this quick stir-fry is completed, turn the heat down to moderate to complete the cooking.

Soft vegetables will be practically cooked already. Stir-fry them for a minute or two until they are just tender, add any seasoning you wish (see below), and remove them with a draining spoon.

Add a little liquid to semi-hard and hard vegetables after the initial stir-frying. In Chinese cooking, no food is ever drowned in liquid, so it must be added sparingly—just enough to create the steam in which the vegetables can finish cooking. Scrape a space on the base of the pan. Pour the liquid on to it, so that it comes into contact with the hot pan before it touches the vegetables. Cover with a lid or foil and steam the vegetables for a few minutes until they are tender. Do not lift the lid during this short stage, for two reasons. One, all the steam would escape, and that is what the vegetables are cooking in. And two, they would lose much of their natural colour. When the vegetables are tender, remove the lid and stir-fry for a moment until all the liquid is absorbed.

SEASONING

Sometimes crushed garlic, thinly-sliced spring onion or thinly-sliced fresh ginger root are cooked in the oil before the vegetables are added. Other seasonings, such as soy sauce, dry sherry or *sake* may be added at the end of the cooking process. They are stir-fried just long enough to coat the vegetables and heat through, but not long enough to soak in and spoil the texture.

Sugar has a very definite affinity to vegetables, particularly the soft ones, and may be stirred in at the end, or combined with vinegar to make a simple sweet-and-sour dressing. This, too, is stirred in for just long enough to heat.

BLANCHING

If it is more convenient, you can blanch semi-hard vegetables the evening or the morning before a dinner party, cool them and store them in the refrigerator. This cuts down precious minutes of cooking time.

Wash and prepare the vegetables, put them in a pan and pour boiling water over them. Or use a vegetable blancher. Stir once or twice, then turn them into a colander or sieve and refresh under cold running water to stop any further cooking. Or you can use frozen vegetables which, when thawed, are treated as blanched ones. Broccoli and green beans are particularly suitable.

ADVANCE COOKING

Since the very essence of Chinese cooking is that fresh ingredients are freshly cooked, it might seem a contradiction to mention advance cooking in this context, but it works perfectly well. Cook the vegetables in the usual way, stir-frying in very hot oil, add the liquid and lower the heat while the vegetables cook in the steam in the covered pan. After the final stirring, leave the vegetables to cool in the *uncovered* pan, away from the heat, then transfer them to a lidded container and store them in the refrigerator. Re-heat them in seconds by stir-frying in very hot oil.

MIXED VEGETABLES

Chinese cooks produce the most marvellous combinations of vegetables with all the excitement that carefully contrasted colours and textures can bring. The vegetables are cooked in the same pan, hard ones that need the longest cooking-time first, then semi-hard ones and lastly the soft vegetables, for the shortest time. The precise cooking times can, of course, be matched a little more closely by slicing the various categories of vegetables more or less thinly than usual, but it does take a little practice to know just when to toss the celery on to the runner beans and how many seconds to count before letting go of the cabbage leaves.

The following recipe is a basic one. You can mix and match the ingredients as different vegetables come into season using, say, garlic, spring onion or ginger for initial flavouring and sugar and other seasonings at the end.

Stir-fried Bean Sprouts

A clove of garlic cooked in the oil adds depth to the flavour of some vegetables but is not essential.

325 g (12 oz) fresh bean sprouts   *3 tbsp vegetable oil*
1 clove garlic (optional)   *½ tsp salt*

1   Wash the bean sprouts in a colander under cold running water and drain them well.
2   Peel and crush the garlic, if used.
3   Heat a heavy-based pan over a fairly high heat. Pour in the oil

with the garlic and salt and wait until the oil starts to sizzle. Toss in the bean sprouts and quickly stir with a wooden spoon to coat them all with the hot oil. Lower the heat to moderate and continue to stir-fry for 2 minutes. Lift the bean sprouts out with a draining spoon and shake them over the pan to release any oil still clinging to them. Put the bean sprouts into a heated serving dish and serve at once.

Using Canned Vegetables

Leaving aside the fairly mundane canned vegetables, one can really come up with some winners from the store-cupboard.

Canned vegetables, which can be served simply by heating in the liquor from the can, are greatly improved with the addition of a little garnish, or a sauce. *Asparagus* is delicious served in a sauce made with half milk and half liquor from the can, or tossed in heated double cream, in butter with a few split almonds turned golden brown, or garnished with a few buttered button mushrooms. Canned *beetroot* can be heated in natural yoghurt, then seasoned lightly with paprika or nutmeg, or be dressed with a swirl of soured cream just before serving. *Broad beans* take well to a crunchy garnish such as crisply-fried bacon cubes, croûtons, chopped walnuts—see the suggestions on page 184. Celery hearts, one of the most versatile of canned vegetables, are delicious served in a white sauce—again, equal quantities of milk and the liquor from the can—and dressed with a generous scattering of celery seed. Or they can be garnished with crisply-fried bacon cubes, chopped walnuts, chopped cooked ham, or grated cheese: put the dish under the grill to brown and bubble the cheese just before serving. Follow the directions on the can to reheat *spinach*, then toss it quickly in very hot, but not browned, butter, or heated double cream and season it well with salt, pepper and nutmeg.

One of my favourites is a dish I make with *canned white haricot beans*. Sauté a sliced onion and two large crushed cloves of garlic in about 75 g (3 oz) butter, then tip in a large tin of the beans, plenty of salt, pepper and chopped parsley. Cover the pot and simmer for 20 minutes or so. The sauce becomes beautifully buttery, garlicky, golden and the vegetables are elevated way above their humble beginnings.

A similar dish is made with canned *flageolets*, those delightfully tender little green beans. Chop a large carrot very small, or slice it very thinly, stir it in plenty of butter with a chopped onion, then add the strained beans and seasoning. A pinch of dried thyme does wonders, too. And the whole thing takes about 2 minutes' working time and 12–15 minutes cooking.

Chick peas, a national favourite in Mediterranean countries, take ages to soak and cook. You can make a very passable vegetable dish by stirring a small can of peeled tomatoes and a tablespoon of tomato purée into an onion-garlic-and-butter sauté. Tip in the drained canned chick peas, season well with salt, pepper and mixed dried herbs, and simmer until the tomatoes form a thick paste enclosing the peas.

I'm always grateful to the canners of *salsify* for doing all the scraping and blanching. Heat up the vegetable in the can liquor, then strain it off (you can use the stock to make a very good white sauce), and add a spoonful or so of double cream.

Apart from serving canned *artichoke hearts* as a first course, I have sometimes used them to stretch a main dish, when people have unexpectedly stayed to a meal that hadn't catered for them—they go particularly well with lamb, pork or veal dishes, especially ones with a creamy sauce. To serve canned artichokes as a vegetable, heat them in the liquor, strain them well, then stir in some double cream, a pinch of allspice and plenty of salt and pepper.

Salads

Don't be too ambitious. Stick to a couple of main ingredients that you personally can prepare in a trice, then add a little something from a can or your store-cupboard—kidney or haricot beans, celery or artichoke hearts, pineapple cubes, mangoes, pears, olives, a handful of raisins, sultanas or nuts.

Another secret is in having a mayonnaise or vinaigrette dressing always on hand. You can make mayonnaise in advance and keep it in the refrigerator for at least a week, longer in an airtight jar, or buy your favourite brand.

Shaking up all the ingredients for a vinaigrette-type dressing in a screw-topped jar or whizzing them in a blender doesn't take a minute, nothing like the care involved in making mayonnaise. But it can be the last straw, so I always keep at least a couple of jars of salad dressing ready made and clearly labelled, perhaps one classic French vinaigrette dressing and one sweetened with honey. For on-the-spot variations, you can fork in some crumbled blue cheese, chopped watercress or other herbs, capers or finely sliced olives.

You will find recipes and ideas for mayonnaise and salad dressings among the other Finishing Touches, beginning on page 168.

There is practically no fruit or vegetable, green or otherwise, that cannot be used in some way for a salad. Here is my list of vegetables that are quick to prepare and accommodatingly versatile on salad days.

Beans

Green beans blanched until barely tender, or thawed frozen ones, are super with raw bean sprouts, drained canned red kidney beans or haricot beans, and with sliced raw mushrooms, anchovy fillets and black olives. Frozen or canned broad beans are good with onion rings and olives, with mushrooms and oregano.

Beetroot

It's rather good grated, mixed with soured cream and served with fresh green salad leaves or cabbage and chopped walnuts.

Cabbage

Good firm cabbages, quick to shred, stay crisp and crunchy for ages. Mix with chopped dates and mayonnaise, with grated raw parsnip and raisins, or sliced banana and sultanas. Good with honey dressing (see page 180).

Carrots

Good with fresh bean sprouts, watercress sprigs and a sweet dressing, or thinly sliced with drained canned celery or artichoke hearts.

Cauliflower

Very small raw or blanched florets, tossed in mayonnaise with walnut halves and raisins or vinaigrette dressing with red kidney beans and spring onion.

Celery

Excellent in mayonnaise with red cabbage and raisins or chopped dates, or cubed cheese and sultanas. In vinaigrette dressing with diced avocado and black olives.

Chicory

Quick to wash and needing no slicing, it combines well with all dark green salad leaves and takes well to all kinds of dressings.

Chinese Leaves or Chinese Cabbage

Served with either mayonnaise or vinaigrette dressings, this makes a very welcome addition to the repertoire of winter salads.

Courgettes

Tiny ones can be sliced very thinly and served raw if they are marinated in a vinaigrette dressing for about half an hour. Good on their own, with fresh chopped parsley or mint, and with finely-snipped spinach, nasturtium or dandelion leaves.

Cucumber

In a yoghurt dressing, it makes a classic side dish to curries and other highly-spiced foods.

Cucumber Raita

1 medium-sized cucumber   *salt*
1 large clove garlic   *1 tbsp chopped mint leaves*
300 ml (½ pt) yoghurt, chilled

1 Wash and trim the cucumber and cut it into small dice. Or, if you prefer, peel and coarsely grate it into a bowl.
2 Peel and crush the garlic.
3 Mix all the ingredients together and serve well chilled.

Endive

Specially good with the deep green contrast of finely snipped raw spinach leaves or tiny sprigs of watercress.

Fennel

Ideal with a main dish that needs a little 'pepping up'. Cut very thinly and combine with spring onions and walnuts, green beans and parsley, grated carrots and canned mushrooms.

Lettuce

Wash the leaves and pat or shake dry, put on one side in the refrigerator and dress at the last minute by coating the leaves first in olive oil, tossing them so that they are thoroughly covered, then adding the vinegar or lemon juice and other seasonings.

Mushrooms

Thinly-sliced raw mushrooms in a garlicky oil dressing are good with both fish and meat dishes. Or try a dressing of yoghurt, cream or soured cream.

Mustard and Cress

Usually sold still growing in little punnets, it's a matter of moments to snip off a handful and wash it in a sieve.

Peppers

Red or green, they can be mixed with all the salad greens, with celery, cabbage, mushrooms, hard-boiled eggs and anchovies and canned vegetables such as celery or artichoke hearts.

Radishes

Useful for colour and crunch—but a bit overpowering, decibel-wise!

Spring Onions

Good with bland ingredients like mushrooms, avocado, courgettes and cucumber.

Sprouting Seeds

Mini saladings worth growing for their creamy-white sprouts are alfalfa, fenugreek and mung beans.

Tomatoes

You needn't make them into a salad at all, just put out a bowl of whole tiny tomatoes. Sliced tomatoes are good with snipped dandelion leaves, olives, chopped spring onions, or basil. Any vinaigrette dressing suits them well, so does yoghurt, cream or soured cream.

Watercress

Cut off all the discoloured bits and wash only the tops that you're going to use. Apart from being a versatile salad ingredient and garnish, it makes a delicious dressing (page 174).

7

PUDDINGS
All recipes serve 6

With under an hour to prepare a meal, most of us think we have performed culinary miracles if we produce a first course and the main dish—never mind a pudding. But some people do mind about a pudding. There are some (ironically, usually the skinniest) who positively yearn all through a meal for that temptingly creamy, gooey something you are going to serve at the end. So if you have dedicated pudding fanciers among you, you might settle for melon or something from the 'deli' for the first course, and go to town to finish the meal on the crest of a wave.

There are, of course, lots of in-a-jiffy puddings that can be served straight from the store-cupboard, such as stem ginger in syrup, green figs, lychees, guavas and goldenberries. And then there is ice-cream. Bought ice-cream takes well to the stirred-in addition of a few chopped nuts, dried fruits, or a hot and fudgy pouring sauce.

If you can borrow a few moments before starting to prepare the meal in earnest, though, you can well be a little more ambitious. If you study a recipe carefully and reckon on putting even a couple of the method steps behind you, the whole thing becomes much more possible. Crush any biscuit or macaroons for decoration or flavouring, grate or crumble chocolate, chop preserved ginger, marshmallows and nuts, toast nuts and coconut, hull fresh soft fruit, squeeze and grate the lemon or orange, weigh dry ingredients like sugar, coconut and dried fruits, and assemble the cans and bottles you will need in a hurry.

And, the day before the meal, check your store-cupboard for the extras you might like to have. All the rich and creamy puddings made with whipped cream, curd or cream cheese or ice-cream are even more enjoyable if there are semi-sweet biscuits to soak up the richness. Ring the changes on sponge finger biscuits, sponge drops, the French cigarettes Russes, brandy snaps, almond biscuits, gingersnaps, shortbread and wafers, which, incidentally, make a little of the pudding go a long way.

Starting from Scratch

Cream Crowdie

A traditional Scots pudding, known as Cranachan.

3 tbsp oatmeal
450 ml (¾ pt) double cream
50 g (2 oz) caster sugar

2 tbsp dark rum
225 g (8 oz) raspberries

1 Spread the oatmeal on a baking tray and toast until it turns just golden brown. Allow to cool.
2 Lightly whip the cream with the sugar and rum until it is frothy.
3 Mix most of the raspberries and toasted oatmeal into the cream.
4 Pour the cream into a serving dish and decorate with the reserved oatmeal and fruit. Serve chilled.

Atholl Brose (See Plate 9)

75 g (3 oz) rolled oats
5 tbsp Scotch whisky
3 rounded tbsp clear honey

1 tsp lemon juice
300 ml (½ pt) double cream
toasted rolled oats to garnish

1 Put oats, whisky, honey and lemon juice into a bowl. Cover and leave to soak for 10–15 minutes, while the oats absorb the flavours.
2 Whip the cream until it is just firm enough to hold its shape.
3 Fold the oats mixture into the cream and pile into 6 glasses. Chill in the refrigerator.
4 Sprinkle with a few toasted rolled oats.

Caledonian Cream

Made on the Scots farms with curd cheese, this pudding tastes very rich.

450 g (1 lb) cottage cheese   *2 tbsp Scotch whisky*
2 heaped tbsp dark marmalade   *1 tbsp lemon juice*
150 g (2 oz) caster sugar

1   Put the cottage cream into a large bowl.
2   Cut up any very large chunks in the marmalade (the least messy
    way to do this is to turn it on to a plate and snip the peel with
    scissors).
3   Beat the marmalade, sugar, whisky and lemon juice into the
    cottage cheese—an electric mixer does it in seconds—until the
    mixture is smooth.
4   Divide the cream between 6 small serving dishes and chill in the
    refrigerator.

Brandy Curds

I often use this filling for Hungarian-style pancakes.

225 g (8 oz) curd cheese   *1 large lemon*
150 ml (5 fl oz) soured cream   *100 g (4 oz) icing sugar*
100 g (4 oz) seedless raisins   *at least 12 brandy snaps*

1   Beat together the curd cheese and soured cream. Beat in the
    raisins.
2   Grate the rind of the lemon. Beat this into the cheese mixture
    and gradually add the sifted icing sugar.
3   Using an icing bag without a nozzle, or just a teaspoon, push
    the filling into brandy snaps and pile up on a serving plate,
    log-cabin fashion.

Marsala Cream

If you do not keep a bottle of 'cooking' Marsala in your cupboard,
use sweet sherry instead.

300 ml ($\frac{1}{2}$ pt) double cream   *100 g (4 oz) caster sugar*
2 lemons (use rind only)   *3 egg whites*
150 ml ($\frac{1}{4}$ pt) Marsala   *25 g (1 oz) ratafias (optional)*

1   Whip the cream until it is stiff.
2   Grate the rind of the lemons.
3   Stir the lemon rind, Marsala and sugar into the cream.
4   Whisk the egg whites until they are stiff and fold them into the
    cream mixture.
5   Spoon the pudding into 6 glasses and chill in the refrigerator.

6   If using ratafias crush them and sprinkle on the pudding to decorate.

Lemon Chantilly Cream

300 ml (½pt) double cream   *40 g (1½oz) caster sugar*
3 egg whites   *1 or 2 small lemons*

1   Whip the cream until it is just stiff.
2   Whisk the egg whites until stiff. Then fold in the caster sugar.
3   Squeeze and strain the juice of the lemon and grate the rind.
4   Lightly stir the juice and rind into the cream, then fold in the egg white mixture.
5   Pile the cream into 6 tall glasses. Serve well chilled. If you have time, decorate each glass with a thin slice of lemon sitting on the rim.

Strawberry Cream

450 g (1 lb) fresh strawberries   *1 tbsp orange Curaçao*
50 g (2 oz) caster sugar   *50 g (2 oz) blanched almonds*
300 ml (½pt) double cream   *(toasted if possible—see page*
2 egg whites   *183)*

1   Hull the strawberries and reserve a few to garnish. Halve the rest, unless they are small. Sprinkle them with sugar.
2   Whip the cream.
3   Whisk the egg whites until stiff.
4   Fold the egg white, liqueur, strawberries and almonds into the cream.
5   Turn the cream into a bowl and serve well chilled, decorated with the reserved strawberries.

When fresh strawberries are not available, frozen raspberries make a good alternative.

Raspberry Syllabub

450 g (1 lb) raspberries (fresh,   *300 ml (½pt) double cream*
   frozen or canned)   *150 ml (¼pt) single cream*
caster sugar (omit if raspberries   *300 ml (½pt) sweet white wine*
   canned)

1   Divide the raspberries between 6 glasses, reserving a few to decorate. Sprinkle them with a little caster sugar. If you use canned raspberries, drain them well; no sugar will be needed.

2   Whip the creams together until stiff.
3   Whip the wine into the cream until it is stiff again.
4   Spoon the cream on to the raspberries and decorate with the
    reserved fruit.

Ginger Syllabub

Be sure that your friends will enjoy this much ginger.

300 ml (½pt) double cream
300 ml (½pt) single cream
1 tbsp brandy
2 tbsp ginger syrup

6 large pieces preserved ginger
25 g (1 oz) blanched almonds
(toasted if possible—see page
183)

1   Whip the creams together until they are stiff, then slowly pour
    on the brandy and ginger syrup, whipping until the mixture
    thickens.
2   Finely chop the preserved ginger and fold this into the cream.
3   Divide the mixture between 6 glasses and scatter them with the
    (toasted) almonds. Serve well chilled.

Hazelnut Mallow

Whisked egg white will 'stretch' yoghurt, giving it a marsh-
mallowy texture.

3 egg whites
75 g (3 oz) caster sugar
2 small cartons hazelnut yoghurt

2 bananas
1 tbsp desiccated coconut (toasted
if possible—see below)

1   Whisk the egg whites until they are stiff.
2   Fold in the caster sugar.
3   Carefully fold in the yoghurt.
4   Peel the bananas and slice them thinly. Fold them into the
    yoghurt mixture.
5   Divide the pudding between 6 glasses and sprinkle with the
    coconut. Toasted coconut combines so much better with the
    'brown' flavours of the yoghurt and takes only seconds in a hot
    oven or under a medium-hot grill.

Chocolate Mallow

Mix and match the various fruit yoghurts with nuts, canned fruit,
dried fruit and crushed biscuits.

3 egg whites
75 g (3 oz) caster sugar
2 small cartons chocolate yoghurt

2 small milk chocolate flake bars
40 g (1½oz) cooking chocolate
'dots'
6 digestive or ginger biscuits

1 Whisk the egg whites until they are stiff.
2 Fold in the caster sugar.
3 Gently fold in the yoghurt.
4 Crumble the chocolate flake bars and fold them into the mixture, with the chocolate dots.
5 Crumble or crush the biscuits.
6 Spoon layers of the chocolate pudding and crushed biscuits into 6 glasses. If you like, sprinkle a few chocolate dots or biscuit crumbs on top. Serve well chilled. You can stick a small chocolate flake bar in the top of each pudding.

Tumbling Peaches

Just provide everyone with the wine and peaches—and a knife and fork to cut up the fruit when the bubbles have subsided.

6 large ripe peaches

1 bottle sparkling white wine, such as Sekt

1 Chill the peaches, the wine and 6 wide-necked glasses.
2 Prick each peach all over with a fork. Just before you start the meal, put a peach into each glass and cover it with wine. Chill in the refrigerator.
3 Top up with more wine as you serve the fruit. Guests sip the wine and tumble the fruit about with a fork. Serve refills of wine as you wish, until eventually the wine-soaked peaches are removed to a pudding plate and eaten.

Peach Velvet

6 large ripe peaches
425-g (15-oz) can blackcurrants
150 ml (¼pt) double cream

25 g (1 oz) almond flakes (toasted if possible—see page 183)
cream, single or soured, to serve (optional)

1 Dip the peaches into boiling water and remove the skins, either by rubbing them off with your fingers, or rolling the skin off

with a sharp knife. Halve the peaches and remove the stones.
2   Drain the blackcurrants and tip them into a shallow serving dish.
3   Arrange the peach halves, cut side up, on the currants and spoon a little of the syrup around them.
4   Whip the cream and fold in the (toasted) almonds. Using a teaspoon, fill the peach halves with the almond cream. Serve well chilled.

Peach Caramels

6 large ripe peaches   *225 g (8 oz) soft dark brown sugar*
30 ml (¼ pt) double cream   *2 tbsp milk*
1 tbsp blanched almond nibs   *25 g (1 oz) butter*

1   Put the peaches in a bowl, cover them with boiling water and leave for a couple of minutes. Rub off the skins, or peel them with a knife. Halve the peaches and remove the stones.
2   Whip the cream and fold in the nibbed almonds. Fill the peaches with the cream and sandwich the halves together again.
3   Put the sugar, milk and butter into a small, heavy saucepan and bring to the boil. Simmer for 7 minutes (you do have to time this) then beat with a wooden spoon until the mixture is thick—just moments.
4   Arrange the peaches in a serving dish and pour the hot caramel sauce over them.

Flaming Peaches

6 large ripe peaches   *caster sugar*
225 g (8 oz) raspberry jam   *6 tbsp brandy*
about 75 g (3 oz) blanched almond
*   nibs*

1   Sieve the raspberry jam on to a plate. If you haven't time to sieve it, it's not the end of the world.
2   Tip the almond nibs on to one sheet of greaseproof paper, the sugar on to another.
3   Roll the peaches in the jam, then in the almond nibs, then in the sugar, to cover them completely.
4   Heat the brandy.

5   Arrange the peaches in a serving dish, pour on the hot brandy
    and flame at the table.

Baked Peaches

6 medium-sized peaches, or 425-g   1 egg yolk
  (15-oz) can peach halves   300 ml (½ pt) sweet white wine
100 g (4 oz) ginger biscuits   6 tbsp clear honey
25 g (1 oz) demerara sugar   1 lemon
25 g (1 oz) butter

1   Dip the fresh peaches into boiling water and rub off skins.
    Halve the peaches and remove the stones, or drain canned
    peaches.
2   Arrange peach halves cut side up in a shallow ovenproof
    dish.
3   Crush the biscuits and mix them with the sugar, butter and egg
    yolk, until smooth.
4   Spoon the biscuit mixture into the peaches and pour on 6
    tablespoons of the wine. Bake at 180°C (350°F), Gas 4, for 20
    minutes.
5   Meanwhile put the honey into a small pan. Squeeze and strain
    the juice and grate the rind of the lemon. Add to the honey with
    the rest of the wine and melt over a low heat. Serve the peaches
    hot with the sauce.

Caramel Pears (See Plate 9)

Cook the pears the night before, and serve them cold. Or cook
them 'on the night' and enjoy them straight from the oven.

6 large firm dessert pears   2 tbsp lemon juice
50 g (2 oz) butter   a pinch of ground cloves
8 tbsp clear honey   whipped double cream, to serve

1   Peel the pears, leaving on the stalk. Stand them upright in a
    fireproof dish.
2   Melt the butter and honey in a small pan. Pour in the lemon
    juice and 'season' with a good pinch of cloves.
3   Pour the hot sauce over the pears and bake at 180°C (350°F),
    Gas 4, for 20–30 minutes, until the pears are just tender. Baste
    the pears with the sauce at intervals when you're passing the
    oven. Serve hot or cold.

Jamaican Meringue

This pudding can cook in the oven while you are eating the main course.

40 g (1½oz) soft dark brown sugar
50 g (2 oz) butter
strained juice of 2 lemons
3 tbsp dark rum
4 egg whites

50 g (2 oz) caster sugar
50 g (2 oz) desiccated coconut
6 bananas
single cream, to serve

1 For the rum sauce, put the brown sugar and butter in a small pan and melt over a low heat. Stir in the lemon juice and rum.
2 To make the meringue, whisk the egg whites until stiff and fold in the caster sugar and coconut.
3 Peel the bananas, cut them in half lengthways and arrange them in a shallow ovenproof dish.
4 Pour over the rum sauce and cover with the meringue, spreading it right out to the sides of the dish. Bake at 170°C (325°F), Gas 3, for 15 minutes, until the meringue is golden brown.

Coconut Bananas

25 g (1 oz) butter
6 bananas
3 tbsp clear honey

50 g (2 oz) desiccated coconut
single cream, to serve (optional)

1 Melt the butter in a shallow fireproof dish.
2 Peel the bananas.
3 Spoon the honey into a shallow dish or a plate.
4 Tip the coconut on to a piece of greaseproof paper.
5 Roll the bananas first in the honey, then in the coconut.
6 Arrange the bananas in the fireproof dish and bake at 170°C (325°F), Gas 3, for 25 minutes. Serve hot, with, if you like, single cream flavoured with a little rum.

Baked Bananas

50 g (2 oz) brandy or rum butter
   (page 172)
2 tbsp brandy or rum
6 bananas

50 g (2 oz) seedless raisins
50 g (2 oz) soft dark brown sugar
single cream, to serve

1 Melt the brandy or rum butter in a shallow fireproof dish in the oven. Stir in the extra brandy or rum.

2   Peel the bananas and halve them lengthways. Arrange them in
    the dish and spoon the butter over them.
3   Scatter the raisins in the dish and sprinkle on the sugar. Bake at
    180 °C (350 °F), Gas 4, for 20–25 minutes. Serve hot. A little extra
    brandy or rum may be sprinkled over the pudding on serving.

Toffee Bananas

A good choice for people who still enjoy 'nursery' puddings.

6 bananas   *40 g (1½ oz) soft dark brown sugar*
175 g (6 oz) dates, chopped   *3 tbsp dark rum*
50 g (2 oz) ground almonds   *2 tbsp lemon juice*

1   Peel the bananas and cut them in half lengthways. Arrange
    them in a shallow ovenproof dish.
2   Mix together the dates, almonds, brown sugar, rum and lemon
    juice and spread it over the fruit.
3   Cover with foil and bake at 180 °C (350 °F), Gas 4, for 20
    minutes. Serve hot.

Bananas in their Jackets

6 bananas   *2 tbsp icing sugar*
4 tbsp Crème de Cacao   *single cream, to serve*

1   Arrange the bananas, in their skins, in a shallow fireproof dish.
    Bake them at 180 °C (350 °F), Gas 4, for 15 minutes.
2   Meanwhile set the liqueur to heat in a small pan.
3   Peel the baked bananas and arrange them in a clean, warm
    dish.
4   Sift on the icing sugar.
5   Pour on the hot liqueur, set light to it and bring the dish to the
    table at once.

Baked Plums

A hot pudding that can also be prepared in advance.

6 thickish slices white bread   *40 g (1½ oz) butter*
450 g (1 lb) plums   *cream, single or soured, to serve*
40 g (1½ oz) sugar

1   Using a large pastry cutter, stamp 6 circles from the bread. Arrange them in a fireproof dish.
2   Wash the plums, remove the stalks, halve them and remove the stones. Arrange the fruit, cut side down, on the bread rounds.
3   Sprinkle the fruit with sugar and dot with butter.
4   Bake at 180°C (350°F), Gas 4, for 20–25 minutes, and serve hot, sprinkled with a little extra sugar.

Greengage Brûlée

Pop this pudding under the grill while you clear the table from the main course, and serve it sizzling.

450 g (1 lb) greengages (canned or   2 egg whites
   frozen)   150 ml ($\frac{1}{4}$ pt) double cream
100 g (4 oz) demerara sugar

1   Drain canned greengages. Halve them and remove the stones. Arrange them cut sides down in an ovenproof dish. Sprinkle with 50 g (2 oz) of the sugar. (You can prepare the fruit to this stage the evening or morning before the meal.)
2   Whisk the egg whites until stiff.
3   Whip the cream until thick.
4   Fold the egg whites into the cream and tip it on to the greengages. Spread it out to reach the sides of the dish.
5   Sprinkle the remaining sugar over the cream and grill under a medium-hot grill for about 4–5 minutes, until the top is golden. Serve hot.

Ice-cream with Hot Rum Sauce

'family-sized' block dark chocolate   50 g (2 oz) butter
   ripple ice-cream   50 g (2 oz) bitter chocolate
3 tbsp black treacle   2 tbsp dark rum

1   Heat the treacle, butter, chocolate and rum together in a small pan.
2   Put the ice-cream block on a serving dish and dribble a very little hot sauce over it. Serve the rest of the sauce in a heated jug.

With a Little Forethought

A few minutes spent the evening or morning before the dinner party can give scope for all those puddings which, although still made in moments, take more time to set or to soften. Here are the creams and mousses that set slowly to a delightful lightness, the 'refrigerator' cakes which take time for the biscuits to soften, and the cooked fruits that must be left to chill.

Yoghurt Ambrosia

This must be left for about 6–8 hours, for the sugar to go syrupy and mingle with the cream.

300 ml (½pt) natural yoghurt
300 ml (½pt) double cream

about 4 tbsp soft light brown
  sugar
extra sugar to serve

1   Whip the yoghurt and cream together until they become light and thick.
2   Pour the cream mixture into 6 ramekin dishes and sprinkle each one fairly thickly with brown sugar.
3   Either put the dishes on a large plate and put the plate inside a plastic bag, or cover each dish with cling film. Leave to chill all day or overnight.
4   Sprinkle each dish with more sugar just before serving.

Burnt Almond Syllabub

The flavour of this pudding is much 'rounder' if you leave the lemon and wine to infuse overnight.

1 small lemon
150 ml (¼ pint) sweet white wine,
  such as Sauternes

75 g (3 oz) caster sugar
300 ml (½pt) double cream
50 g (2 oz) toasted almond flakes

1   Thinly pare the rind from the lemon without including any pith. Squeeze the juice.
2   Put the lemon rind and juice into a bowl with the wine and if possible leave, covered, overnight.
3   Stir in the sugar to dissolve it. Remove the lemon rind.
4   Add the cream to the bowl and beat until it is just stiff and will stand in peaks.
5   Fold in the almond flakes, reserving a few for decoration.
6   Divide the pudding between 6 small ramekin dishes and decorate each with a pinch of almonds. Serve well chilled.

Cider Syllabub

150 ml (¼ pt) dry cider
1 tbsp brandy
1 lemon

50 g (2 oz) caster sugar
½ tsp grated nutmeg
300 ml (½ pt) double cream

1   Thinly pare the rind of the lemon and put it in a bowl with the cider and brandy. Cover and leave overnight.
2   Strain the liquor into a bowl and add the sugar and nutmeg, stirring. Remove the lemon rind.
3   Add the cream slowly and whisk until thick.
4   Spoon into 6 glasses and chill in the refrigerator for as long as time allows—while the meal is in progress.

Zabaglione Cream

4 egg yolks
2 tbsp water
100 ml (3½ fl oz) Marsala

50 g (2 oz) caster sugar
150 ml (¼ pt) double cream
ratafias to decorate (optional)

1   Put the egg yolks, water, Marsala and caster sugar in a basin over hot water or in the warmed bowl of an electric mixer. Whisk until the mixture is thick and fluffy.
2   Stand the bowl in cold water to reduce the temperature quickly. Whisk for 2–3 minutes more, when the mixture should be at blood heat.
3   Whip the cream and fold it into the egg mixture. Pour into a serving dish and refrigerate overnight.
4   Decorate the dish if you like with a handful of ratafias.

Ricotta al Caffè

450 g (1 lb) ricotta cheese (or use
curd or low-fat cream cheese:
not cottage cheese)
100 g (4 oz) caster sugar

25 g (1 oz) fine ground coffee
2 tbsp brandy
brandy snaps, to serve

1 Sieve the cheese.
2 Add the caster sugar and sift in the coffee through a fine sieve (any 'grits' in the coffee ruin both texture and flavour). Add the brandy and beat well with an electric beater until the cream is smooth.
3 Cover the bowl and leave the cheese to chill, and the flavours to blend, overnight or all day.

Ratafia Cream

225 g (8 oz) macaroons
2 egg yolks
75 g (3 oz) icing sugar

4 tbsp dark rum
1 tsp ratafia
300 ml (½ pt) double cream

1 Crumble the macaroons or reduce them to coarse crumbs in a blender. Put them in a bowl.
2 Whip together the egg yolks, sifted icing sugar, rum and ratafia until the mixture is pale. Pour it over the macaroons, cover and leave to soak for 15 minutes.
3 Whip the cream until it is smooth and fold in the macaroon mixture. Turn into a serving dish and put in the refrigerator to set and chill—allow a couple of hours.

Coeur à la Crème

225 g (8 oz) cottage cheese
300 ml (½ pt) double cream
2 tbsp icing sugar

450 g (1 lb) strawberries
caster sugar
single cream, to serve

1 Sieve the cottage cheese into a bowl.
2 Stir in the cream, sift in the icing sugar and beat well.
3 Line a sieve with a piece of muslin, tip in the cream mixture and drain over a bowl overnight.
4 Serve the cream in little moulds or pretty ramekin dishes with the hulled strawberries. Serve caster sugar separately.

Pink Strawberry Cream

675 g (1½ lb) fresh strawberries   *50–75 g (2–3 oz) caster sugar*
600 ml (1 pt) double cream

1 Hull the strawberries. Cut large ones in half.
2 Whip the cream until it is just stiffening, but still floppy.
3 Gradually add the strawberries to the cream, stirring them so
   that they crush slightly (this will colour the cream pink).
4 When all the strawberries have been added, turn the cream into
   a serving bowl and leave it in the refrigerator to chill—all day if
   necessary, but it must be at least 1 hour.
5 Just before serving, sprinkle the top with the caster sugar.

Chocolate Mousse

The boiling cream melts the chocolate and cooks the egg, then you
just leave the mousse to set.

200 g (7 oz) bitter chocolate   *300 ml (½ pt) single cream*
1 orange   *a pinch of salt*
1 vanilla pod   *1 egg*

1 Break up the chocolate and put it in a blender bowl.
2 Grate the rind of the orange.
3 Heat the cream with the vanilla pod until it is boiling.
4 Remove the vanilla pod (wash and dry it to use again) and pour
   the cream into the blender. Blend until smooth.
5 Add a pinch of salt, the grated orange rind and the egg and
   blend again until the mousse is smooth.
6 Pour the mousse into 6 individual chocolate cups or ramekin
   dishes, allow to cool, then leave overnight or all day in the
   refrigerator—the mousse will set to a light, slightly runny consistency.

Chestnut Chocolate Berg

This is acceptably quick to make as long as you have an electric
mixer.

100 g (4 oz) bitter chocolate   *2 eggs*
75 ml (2½ fl oz) water   *175 g (6 oz) softened butter*
75 g (3 oz) caster sugar   *chocolate buttons, flake, dots or*
425-g (15-oz) can unsweetened   *vermicelli to decorate (optional)*
* chestnut purée*   *double cream, to serve*

1   Break up the chocolate and melt it in a pan with the water and sugar, stirring occasionally.
2   Turn the chestnut purée into a bowl, beat to break it up, and beat in the slightly cooled chocolate mixture.
3   Separate the eggs. Beat the yolks and butter into the chestnut.
4   Whisk the egg whites until stiff, and fold them into the mixture.
5   Turn the pudding into a serving dish and leave in the refrigerator to set. If you like, scatter the top with a chocolate decoration.

Chocolate Cherry Layer

If you have an electric mixer the two beating operations are done in a trice. The rest is just like making a sandwich.

165 g (5½ oz) chocolate wafer
  biscuits
50 g (2 oz) butter
100 g (4 oz) icing sugar

1 egg yolk
300-g (11-oz) can cherry pie
  filling
150 ml (¼ pt) double cream
single cream, to serve

1   Crush the biscuits by putting them in a polythene bag and rolling them with a rolling pin, or by crushing them in a blender.
2   Spread half of the crumbs in the base of a non-stick tin 20 cm (8 in) square.
3   Cream together the butter and sifted icing sugar until light and fluffy, then beat in the egg yolk.
4   Spread the butter cream over the crumbs in the tin, and cover with the pie filling, smoothing it out with a knife.
5   Whip the cream until stiff and spread this over the pie filling.
6   Finish with a layer of the remaining biscuit crumbs, pressed well down. Chill overnight.

Chocolate Rum Cake (See Plate 9)

225 g (8 oz) digestive biscuits
225 g (8 oz) bitter chocolate
225 g (8 oz) butter
2 eggs
50 g (2 oz) caster sugar

50 g (2 oz) walnuts, chopped
40 g (1½ oz) mixed candied peel,
  chopped
3 tbsp rum
walnut halves to decorate

1   Crush the digestive biscuits to coarse crumbs, either with a rolling pin or in a blender.

2   Melt the chocolate and butter together over a pan of hot water.
3   Beat the eggs and sugar together until they are light, then beat in the chocolate butter.
4   Fold in the chopped walnuts and candied peel and stir in the rum and biscuit crumbs.
5   Grease a cake tin with a push-out base and turn the cake mixture into it. Leave overnight in the refrigerator to set.

Ginger Cream Cake

300 ml (½ pt) double cream   *2 pieces preserved ginger*
2 tbsp ginger syrup   *225 g (8 oz) ginger biscuits*

1   Whip the cream until stiff and whip in the ginger syrup.
2   Cut 3 or 4 slices of preserved ginger to decorate, and chop the rest finely.
3   Fold the chopped ginger into the cream.
4   Spread each gingernut biscuit with the ginger cream and make 2 piles, side by side, to give a figure 8 shape.
5   Cover the cake with the rest of the cream, roughing it up with a fork. Arrange the reserved ginger slices on top. Cover the cake loosely with foil and refrigerate for at least 6–8 hours so that the cream softens the biscuits. It will then be easy to cut it through in striped slices.

Oranges in Liqueur

6 medium-sized oranges   *double cream, to serve*
orange Curaçao, or other orange
  liqueur

1   Dip the oranges in boiling water, then peel them and slice each one thinly over a plate to catch the juice.
2   Arrange the orange slices in a shallow dish, pour on any juice and sprinkle with about 6 tablespoons of the liqueur. Cover the dish and leave for several hours in the refrigerator. Turn the fruit at least once in the liqueur before serving.
3   Sprinkle with a little more liqueur.

Tipsy Summer Pudding

Reminiscent of traditional summer pudding, but a great deal quicker to prepare.

8 trifle sponge cakes
4 tbsp sweet sherry
425-g (15-oz) can raspberries
3 tbsp clear honey

300 ml (½ pt) double cream
25 g (1 oz) blanched almonds
  (optional)

1 Break up the sponge cakes into a bowl.
2 Pour on the sherry.
3 Drain the raspberries and add them to the bowl. Measure 6 tablespoons of the juice into a small pan, add the honey and heat just enough to melt it.
4 Pour the honey mixture into the bowl and stir well. Either turn the fruit mixture into a 600-ml (1-pint) pudding basin (to turn it out later) or into a serving dish. Put a plate on top of the pudding to rest on the surface. Put a weight on top and leave overnight in the refrigerator.
5 If you used a basin, turn the pudding out on to a serving dish. Swirl a little cream on top and scatter with the almonds if used. Serve the rest of the cream separately.

Bilberry Cream Flan

300 ml (½ pt) double cream
50 g (2 oz) caster sugar
5 tbsp medium sherry
1 lemon

375-g (14-oz) can bilberry pie
  filling
1 sponge flan case
blanched almonds (optional)

1 Whip together the cream and caster sugar and beat in the sherry.
2 Squeeze the juice and grate the rind of the lemon. Add this to the cream and beat until thick.
3 Beat in half the pie filling. Pour into the flan ring and chill in the refrigerator overnight or all day.
4 Spread the remaining pie filling over the top and decorate, if you wish, with blanched almonds.

Strawberry Frippery

450 g (1 lb) fresh strawberries
40 g (1½ oz) caster sugar
2 tbsp Kirsch
1 tbsp Maraschino

'family-sized' dairy cream
  ice-cream
150 ml (¼ pt) double cream, to
  decorate (optional)

1 Hull the strawberries and put them in a bowl with the sugar and liqueurs. Stir carefully with a wooden spoon. Cover and leave

in the refrigerator overnight, or as long as possible before the meal.
2   Divide the ice-cream between 6 glasses or fruit bowls and spoon the strawberry mixture over.
3   If using cream, whip it lightly and put swirls on top of the fruit.

Ice-cream with Fruit and Nut Sauce

You can make the sauce a day or two before. If you like, add still more interest by flaming it at the table.

150 ml (¼ pt) water
100 g (4 oz) sugar
50 g (2 oz) blanched chopped almonds
50 g (2 oz) glacé cherries

100 g (4 oz) mincemeat
6 cubes sugar ⎫ optional
real lemon extract ⎬
'family-sized' dairy cream ice-cream

1   Put the water and sugar in a small pan, stir to dissolve the sugar, bring to the boil, and boil for 5 minutes.
2   Chop and stir in the cherries, stir in the chopped almonds, add the mincemeat. Mix well and allow the sauce to cool.
3   Divide the ice-cream between 6 serving dishes and pour the sauce over.
4   If you want to flame the dish, dip the sugar lumps in extract of lemon and put one on each dish. Light the sugar cubes with a match.

Brandy Plums

A very little brandy added to the syrup gives the illusion of plums preserved in lots of it.

675 g (1½ lb) firm plums
100 g (4 oz) sugar
300 ml (½ pt) water
2 tbsp brandy

40 g (1½ oz) blanched almonds
soured cream, to serve (optional)
a pinch of ground cinnamon (optional)

1   Wash the plums and remove any stalks.
2   Put the sugar and water in a pan and bring to the boil. Stir to dissolve the sugar.
3   Add the brandy and the plums to the syrup and simmer over a low heat for a few minutes until the fruit is just tender, but not broken. (The exact time will depend on the size and ripeness of the plums.)
4   Stir in the almonds and leave to cool. Serve well chilled.

5   If using soured cream, lightly beat it with a good pinch of
    cinnamon and serve it separately.

Dried Fruit Salad

450 g (1 lb) mixed dried fruit, e.g.   *100 g (4 oz) sugar*
prunes, apples, pears, apricots,   *1 lemon*
nectarines, peaches   *½ tsp ground cinnamon*
100 g (4 oz) seedless raisins   *a pinch of powdered clove*
900 ml (1½ pts) water   *1 tbsp brandy*

1   In the morning, put all the dried fruit to soak in the water.
2   That evening, strain the water into a pan with the sugar.
3   Squeeze the juice of the lemon and thinly pare the rind. Add
    this to the pan with the spices. Bring to the boil and simmer for
    10 minutes.
4   Simmer the fruit until it is just tender. Remove the lemon rind
    and stir in the brandy. Allow to cool.
5   Leave overnight in the refrigerator.

Cranberry Pears

6 large pears   *150 ml (¼ pt) double cream*
275 g (10 oz) can or bottle whole   *(optional)*
cranberry sauce   *pistachios or toasted almonds, to*
90 ml (3 fl oz) red wine   *decorate (optional)*
¼ tsp ground cinnamon

1   Peel the pears, cut them in half and remove the core.
2   Put the cranberry sauce, red wine and cinnamon in a wide pan
    and lightly poach the pears over a low heat for 15–20 minutes,
    until they are tender.
3   Transfer the pears, cut side down, on to a serving plate. Allow
    the cranberry syrup to cool in the pan, then pour it over the
    fruit.
4   If you are serving cream, whip and swirl it over the pears, and,
    if you like, scatter it with nuts. Serve well chilled.

You can poach whole peeled and cored apples in cranberry sauce in
the same way.

Mainly from Store

Danish Peasant Pudding

2 375-g (14-oz) cans apple pie
    filling
175 g (6 oz) rye bread
50 g (2 oz) butter

50 g (2 oz) demerara sugar
150 ml ($\frac{1}{4}$ pt) double cream
1 chocolate flake bar (optional)

1   Grate the rye bread or crumb it in a blender.
2   Melt the butter in a frying-pan, stir in the crumbs and sugar and fry over a moderate heat for 4–5 minutes, until dry. Leave to cool.
3   Choose a glass serving bowl—a straight-sided one is traditional—and spread a layer of apple filling.
4   Make alternate layers of apple and crumbs, finishing with the fruit.
5   Whip the cream lightly and spread it over the dish. If using a chocolate bar, crumble it on top. Serve well chilled.

Berry Compote

2 425-g (15-oz) cans raspberries
425-g (15-oz) can redcurrants
3 tbsp arrowroot
1 tbsp Kirsch

150 ml (5 fl oz) soured cream
blanched almonds, preferably
    toasted—see p. 183 (optional)

1   Purée the raspberries and redcurrants in a blender.
2   Mix the arrowroot with a little of the purée, to make a smooth paste.
3   Bring the purée to the boil in a saucepan, then stir in the arrowroot and the Kirsch. Return to the boil, stirring, and simmer for 3 minutes. Allow to cool.
4   Pour into a serving dish and pour on soured cream to cover the top. Decorate, if you wish, with toasted almonds.

Cherry Sour

375-g (14-oz) can cherry pie
   filling
3 tbsp Kirsch
1 small carton natural yoghurt

4 large macaroons
40 g (1½oz) demerara sugar
150 ml (5 fl oz) soured cream
cinnamon (optional)

1 Tip the cherry pie filling into a bowl and stir in the Kirsch and the yoghurt until thoroughly blended.
2 Crush the macaroons or put them in a blender just long enough to give coarse crumbs, not powder.
3 Mix the crumbs with the sugar.
4 Starting and finishing with the fruit, spoon alternate layers of cherry filling and crumbs into 6 tall glasses.
5 Put 1 tablespoon of soured cream on top of each glass and tip it so that the cream covers the surface. Sprinkle, if you like, with a pinch of cinnamon to decorate.

Black Cherry Cream

375-g (14-oz) can cherry pie
   filling
2 tbsp Kirsch
300 ml (½pt) double cream

2 tbsp natural yoghurt
200-g (7-oz) can black cherries
40 g (1½oz) bitter chocolate

1 Stir the Kirsch into the cherry pie filling.
2 Whip the cream until it is stiff, then beat in the yoghurt.
3 Stir the cherry mixture into the cream and turn into a serving bowl.
4 Drain the cherries.
5 Grate the chocolate—using a blender for speed.
6 Sprinkle the chocolate on top of the pudding and arrange the cherries in a pattern.

Chestnut Cream

425-g (15-oz) can unsweetened
   chestnut purée
75 g (3 oz) icing sugar

2 tbsp sweet sherry
300 ml (½pt) double cream
chocolate dots, to decorate

1 Turn the chestnut purée into a bowl and beat until it is smooth—an electric mixer of course does it in moments.
2 Sift in the icing sugar, add the sherry and beat until the purée is smooth again.

3   Whip the cream. Reserve a little to decorate and slowly beat the
    rest into the chestnut mixture.
4   Turn the pudding into a serving dish and chill for as long as
    possible. Decorate with swirls of whipped cream and a few
    chocolate dots.

Mandarin Orange Ambrosia

40 g (1½oz) desiccated coconut   *100 g (4 oz) pink and white*
300 ml (½pt) double cream   *   marshmallows*
150 ml (5 fl oz) soured cream   *215-g (7½-oz) can mandarin*
                                               *   oranges*
    marshmallows

1   Spread the coconut on to a baking tray and toast in a hot oven or
    under a grill until light brown.
2   Whip the double cream until it is stiff. Then fold in the soured
    cream.
3   Reserving a little to decorate, fold the toasted coconut into the
    cream.
4   If the marshmallows are large ones, cut them in half. Fold them
    into the cream.
5   Arrange layers of mandarin oranges and marshmallow cream
    in 6 glasses. Top each with a sprinkling of coconut and a few
    orange segments.

Refined Chocolate Pudding

2 pkts instant chocolate pudding   *300 ml (½pt) single cream*
2 tsp instant coffee powder   *2 eggs*
300 ml (½pt) milk   *2 milk chocolate flake bars*

1   Add the coffee powder to the chocolate pudding mix and make
    up according to the directions on the packet, but using half milk
    and half single cream.
2   Separate the eggs. Whip in the egg yolks and beat until smooth.
    Whisk the egg whites and fold them in.
3   Divide the pudding between 6 glasses.
4   Cut the chocolate flake bars into 3 sections and decorate each
    glass with one.

Ice-cream with Planet Sauce

'family-sized' block dairy cream   *40 g (1½ oz) chocolate cooking dots*
  ice-cream   *3 Mars bars*
50 g (2 oz) chopped hazelnuts

1   Put the ice-cream block into a bowl and break it up a little with a fork or wooden spoon.
2   Stir in most of the chopped nuts and chocolate dots, reserving a few of each. Return the ice-cream to the freezing compartment of the refrigerator.
3   Melt the Mars bars in a small pan over a low heat. When ready to serve, turn the ice-cream into a serving bowl and sprinkle with the reserved nuts and chocolate dots. Pour the hot fudge-like sauce into a serving boat.

8

FINISHING TOUCHES

On a good day, when no one's coming to dinner and it's too wet to mow the lawn, take time to build up a stock of home-made flavourings, dressings and toppings so that each dish you serve has your own individual stamp, right down to the last detail.

Herbs

When food is quickly and simply cooked—fast food—flavouring is more important than ever. The ingredients in a sauce, dressing or topping have little chance to blend and mellow, and so I like to use fresh herbs whenever possible, and there is nothing to compare with them for instant garnishes.

It isn't difficult to grow herbs in the kitchen. They flourish even in cold, draughty spots, though a south-facing window sill is ideal. If you do not want the job of raising seeds, you can buy tiny plants from a garden centre or herbalist.

Parsley can be planted two or three seedlings to a tiny pot. As you cut the older leaves, new ones will grow. *Chives*, a perennial grown from bulbs, will obligingly produce new shoots to replace all those you cut. *Mint*: to stop it getting straggly, pinch out the tops of the shoots. As soon as a shoot has five or six pairs of leaves, snip off the top three pairs—a fine sprig for a garnish. *Sage* and *thyme* need to be kept slightly moist. Pick off the most mature leaves to allow new ones to develop.

Flavoured Butters

Herb, spice and other flavoured butters are marvellously versatile. A pat of *maître d'hôtel* butter gliding over the surface of grilled steak or chops, releasing colourful herbs as it melts; mustard butter bringing sparkle and spiciness to grilled fish, or garlic butter impregnating a pan of mushrooms, are finishing touches that imply far more preparation than they take.

Flavoured butters are quick and easy to make, using a blender or electric mixer, and can be used as a garnish or cooking fat at a moment's notice. They can also be served with hot crusty rolls or French bread to accompany soup or pasta.

The method for all these butters, some so well known that they have taken their place among the classic dishes, is the same.

Maître d'Hôtel Butter—Basic Recipe

This simple parsley butter, one of the classics, is a typical example. It can be served with grilled meat or fish, potatoes or green vegetables. Shaped into a roll and closely wrapped in foil, it will keep for one month in the refrigerator or several months in the freezer.

You can make various herb butters in the same way. Try using chopped fresh mint, rosemary, watercress or chives.

225 g (8 oz) unsalted butter   *1 tbsp lemon juice*
4 heaped tbsp fresh parsley leaves

Blender method
If you have a blender, there is no need to chop herbs or crush garlic; the machine will do it for you.

1   Cut the butter into pieces and blend it at low speed until it is smooth. Stop the machine and scrape the butter away from the sides if necessary.
2   When the butter is creamed, add the parsley leaves and lemon juice and blend on high speed until the parsley is chopped.

Electric mixer method
1   Chop the parsley. Cut the butter into pieces.
2   Warm the mixer bowl and beater and cream the butter on a slow speed.
3   When it is creamed, add the chopped parsley and lemon juice and increase the speed. Beat until well blended.

Storing
Shape the butter into a roll, wrap it closely in foil and chill it in the refrigerator (or store in a freezer). Cut off round slices to serve.

Ravigote (Mixed Herb) Butter

Herb garden enthusiasts can be proud to serve this butter, a medley of summer fragrances, with grilled meat or fish.

225 g (8 oz) unsalted butter
heaped tbsp each of parsley,
tarragon, chive and chervil
leaves

1 small onion, peeled and chopped
(for blender), or grated (for
mixer)

Garlic Butter

Sometimes called 'Snail Butter', this can be used to cook mushrooms, and is usually served with baked mussels and other shellfish, also to garnish grilled meat, especially steak. A similar butter, without the onion, is used to flavour crisp, hot French loaves.

225 g (8 oz) butter
3 large cloves garlic, peeled. Crush
for mixer method
1 small onion, peeled. Grate for
mixer method

salt
freshly ground black pepper
4 tbsp chopped parsley leaves

French Bread with Garlic or Other Savoury Butters

Make deep slanting cuts into the loaf at 3·5-cm (1½-in) intervals, without cutting right through. Spread the butter on both sides of each slice. Wrap the loaf tightly in foil and heat it in the oven at 200 °C (400 °F), Gas 6, for 15–20 minutes, until the butter has melted and the loaf is hot and crispy.

Mustard Butter

Use this one with oily fish, such as herring and mackerel. The spice offsets the richness of the fish.

225 g (8 oz) butter
2 tbsp French mustard

salt
freshly ground black pepper

Anchovy Butter

Particularly good with grilled white fish, and with grilled steak.

225 g (8 oz) unsalted butter
50-g (1¾-oz) can anchovy fillets,
drained. Mash for mixer
method

1 tsp lemon juice

Orange Butter

With grilled pork chops, baked pork fillet, veal and grilled fish.

225 g (8 oz) unsalted butter　　　　*1 tbsp tomato purée*
2 Seville oranges, juice and grated
　rind

Yorkshire Butter

Take advantage of the combined flavours of fruit and spices in a
bottled sauce. Good with steak, chops or white fish.

100 g (4 oz) unsalted butter　　　　*2 tsp lemon juice*
2 tsp thick Yorkshire Relish　　　　*salt*
2 tbsp parsley leaves. Chop for　　　*a pinch of cayenne pepper*
　mixer method

Curried Butter

Serve this spicy butter on grilled steak or white fish, or glistening
the top of rice to accompany curry.

100 g (4 oz) unsalted butter　　　　*a pinch of cayenne pepper*
1 rounded tsp curry powder　　　　*1 tsp lemon juice*
a good pinch of ground ginger

Quick Spiced Butters

Instead of blending the flavouring into the butter, you can serve
colourful pats or slices of butter simply dipped in the spice. To do
this, have the butter well chilled. Cut it into slices of about 15 g
($\frac{1}{2}$ oz). Put the ground spice into a saucer or a piece of greaseproof
paper and turn or toss each slice to coat it thoroughly. Mild paprika
powder or curry powder are specially good, and can be served with
rice or pasta. Cinnamon butter, made in the same way, can be
served with rice pudding or bread and butter pudding.

Brandy or Rum Butter

To serve with fruit pancakes, waffles, baked bananas and bread
and butter pudding.

225 g (8 oz) unsalted butter　　　　*6 tbsp brandy or rum*
225 g (8 oz) sifted icing sugar, or
　soft light brown sugar

1 Cut the butter into pieces.
2 Warm the mixer bowl and beater of the electric mixer (or a mixing bowl). Cream the butter at medium speed on the mixer, or beat it with a wooden spoon.
3 Gradually add the sugar and continue beating until smooth and fluffy.
4 Add the brandy or rum gradually, still beating, until it is thoroughly blended.

Sauces

Blender Mayonnaise

With a blender, you can make this basic mayonnaise and several variations, to serve with salad, vegetables, meat (including fondue bourguignonne) or fish. An alternative recipe is given for use with an electric mixer.

1 egg, at room temperature
1 tbsp white wine vinegar
1 tsp caster sugar
½ tsp salt
¼ tsp ground white pepper

¼ tsp mustard powder
300 ml (½ pt) olive or other
  vegetable oil at room
  temperature

1 Put all the ingredients except the oil into the blender. Cover and blend at medium speed for 5 seconds. Keep the machine running and gradually pour in the oil through the hole in the lid until it is all incorporated—about 1 minute.
2 Store the mayonnaise in a screw-top jar in the refrigerator. It will keep for up to 4 weeks in an airtight container.

Mustard Mayonnaise

Using two egg yolks instead of a whole egg, this is a thicker mixture. It is very good with oily fish and with green vegetables.

2 egg yolks
2 tsp Dijon mustard
½ tsp salt

¼ tsp ground white pepper
1 tsp lemon juice
300 ml (½ pt) olive oil

Put the egg yolks into the blender with the mustard, salt, pepper and lemon juice. Cover and blend at medium speed for 5 seconds. Gradually pour in the oil through the hole in the lid and continue blending for about 1 minute, until it is all incorporated.

Tomato Mayonnaise

Use this variation for seafood salads.

1 basic recipe mayonnaise   2 tsp Worcestershire sauce
1 dsp tomato purée

Blend the tomato purée and Worcestershire sauce into the mayonnaise.

Belvedere Sauce

A strong-flavoured mayonnaise to serve with cold meats.

1 basic recipe mayonnaise   1 tsp chives
1 tbsp tomato purée   50 g (2 oz) Danish Blue cheese,
a pinch of dried mint   crumbled

Blend the remaining ingredients with the mayonnaise until the sauce is smooth.

Watercress Mayonnaise

Serve with salmon, salmon trout, trout, or avocado pears.

1 basic recipe mayonnaise   2 cloves garlic
2 bunches watercress   1 dsp lemon juice

1 Cut off and discard most of the stalk from the watercress. Wash and dry the tops.
2 Peel the garlic and cut the cloves in half.
3 Put the watercress, garlic and lemon juice into the blender and blend to a paste.
4 Stir or blend into mayonnaise, and chill.

Green Mayonnaise

To serve with fish or salads.

1 basic recipe mayonnaise   1 tbsp parsley
1 clove garlic   1 tbsp tarragon leaves
1 tbsp chives

1 Peel the garlic clove and cut it in half.
2 Add the garlic and herbs to the mayonnaise and blend until smooth.

Pimento Mayonnaise

A perfect complement to a salad accompanying a chicken dish.

1 basic recipe mayonnaise *2 canned red pimentos*

Roughly chop the pimentos and liquidize them in the blender. Blend into the mayonnaise.

Mixer Mayonnaise

With all liaison sauces, such as mayonnaise, it is important to have all the ingredients at room temperature. Eggs taken straight from the refrigerator, or chilly vegetable oil will lead to curdling.

2 egg yolks, at room temperature *300 ml (½pt) olive or other*
½ tsp salt *vegetable oil*
¼ tsp ground white pepper *1 tbsp lemon juice*
¼ tsp mustard powder

1 Put the egg yolks in the mixer bowl with the salt, pepper and mustard and mix at high speed for 10 seconds.
2 Reduce the speed to medium and gradually pour in the oil, very slowly at first.
3 When the oil has been nearly absorbed, add the lemon juice, increase the speed and mix until thick.

Tartare Sauce

To serve with fish.

1 basic recipe mayonnaise *4 medium-sized gherkins*
2 tsp capers *1 tbsp parsley*
2 medium-sized pickled onions *8 stuffed green olives*

1 Roughly chop the onions, gherkins and olives.
2 Add all the remaining ingredients to the mayonnaise and blend until they are coarsely chopped. The mixture should not be smooth.

Blender Hollandaise Sauce

The conventional way of making hollandaise has nothing to offer 60-minute cooks—all that whisking over a pan of hot water, and adding the butter cube by cube. Try this method. It's a perfect hot sauce for asparagus and broccoli.

100 g (4 oz) unsalted butter   *1 tbsp warm water*
3 egg yolks   *salt and white pepper*
1 tbsp lemon juice

1   Melt the butter in a small pan.
2   Put the egg yolks, lemon juice, water and seasoning into the blender. Cover and blend at low speed for 5 seconds. Gradually pour the melted butter through the hole in the lid until it is all absorbed. Switch off the blender at once. Ideally, serve the sauce immediately, before the butter sets. But you can keep it warm in a pan of hot (not boiling) water or a wide-necked vacuum flask.

Maltaise Sauce

Hollandaise sauce flavoured with orange is good with vegetables, particularly cauliflower and broccoli.

1 basic recipe hollandaise sauce   *1 small orange*

1   Squeeze the juice of the orange and grate half the rind.
2   Blend these into the hollandaise sauce. Serve it hot.

Mustard Hollandaise Sauce

A smooth but spicy sauce to serve hot with fish.

100 g (4 oz) unsalted butter   *2 tsp warm water*
2 egg yolks   *salt and white pepper*
1 tsp lemon juice   *1 tbsp Dijon mustard*

1   Melt the butter in a small pan.
2   Follow the directions for basic blender hollandaise sauce, adding the mustard at the end.
3   You can keep the sauce warm until serving by standing it in a pan of hot water.

Mousseline Sauce

With the addition of cream, it is richer yet lighter than hollandaise sauce—to serve hot with fish.

1 recipe basic hollandaise sauce   *150 ml ($\frac{1}{4}$ pt) double cream*

1 Transfer the made hollandaise sauce into a bowl.
2 Blend the cream in the blender, then fold it into the sauce. Add more seasoning if required. Keep the sauce hot in a pan of hot water.

Horseradish Cream

This chilled, spiced cream can be served with grilled steak or oily fish such as mackerel.

150 ml (¼ pt) double cream
1 tbsp horseradish relish
1 tsp lemon juice
2 tsp Worcestershire sauce
1 pinch of salt
2 spring onions

1 Trim and peel the onions, discarding most of the green tops. Roughly cut up the white part.
2 Put all the ingredients into the blender and blend at medium speed until the onions are finely chopped.
3 Chill the cream in a covered container in the refrigerator. Serve it on steaks in mini balls scooped out with a melon baller or teaspoon.

Mustard Cream

Serve with fish, green vegetables or jacket potatoes.

150 ml (¼ pt) double cream
1 heaped tsp parsley leaves
1 tbsp German mustard

1 Blend all the ingredients together until the parsley is finely chopped.
2 Chill in a covered container in the refrigerator.

Danish Grill Sauce

With the unmistakable 'bite' of Danish Blue cheese, an instant sauce to garnish grilled steak. Also good with spring onions.

100 g (4 oz) cottage cheese
2 tbsp white wine vinegar
1 tsp caster sugar
½ tsp mustard powder
50 g (2 oz) Danish Blue cheese, crumbled
1 tsp chives

Blend all the ingredients together at high speed. Store in a covered container in the refrigerator.

Basic Vinaigrette Dressing

This is a basic recipe to make French dressing in a blender. Without a blender, shake all the ingredients together vigorously in a jar until they are cloudy. Shake again before using. It will keep for several weeks in a screw-topped jar or lidded polythene container.

300 ml (½ pt) olive or other salad oil
150 ml (¼ pt) white wine vinegar
1 tsp salt
½ tsp freshly ground black pepper
1 tsp caster sugar
1 tsp mustard powder

Put all the ingredients into a blender, cover, and blend at maximum speed.

Variations
Use any other flavoured vinegar, such as red wine, cider, tarragon or garlic vinegar or replace some of the vinegar with lemon juice. To enhance the flavour, store a sprig of fresh rosemary or tarragon or a peeled and halved clove of garlic, or a good pinch of mixed dried herbs, in the vinaigrette dressing.

Herb Dressing

As well as storing a sprig of fresh herb or a pinch of dried herbs in the vinaigrette dressing, you can add more flavour—and colour—by stirring in chopped fresh herbs just before serving. Add the herbs in the proportion of 2 tablespoons fresh chopped herbs to the basic dressing (300 ml, ½ pint, of oil). Try watercress, parsley, mint, chives, tarragon, chervil or marjoram leaves alone, or mix two or more herbs as you wish.

Curry Dressing

Add 1 tsp curry powder to basic ingredients for vinaigrette dressing and blend. Stir in 2 finely chopped spring onions.

Horseradish Dressing

Blend 1 tbsp horseradish cream with basic ingredients for vinaigrette dressing.

Chutney Dressing

Blend 1 tbsp chutney sauce with basic ingredients for vinaigrette dressing, then stir in 1 tbsp chopped mango chutney.

Slimmer's Dressing

135-ml (4½-fl oz) can fresh tomato
   juice
1 tbsp Worcestershire sauce
2 tbsp lemon juice

salt
freshly ground black pepper
1 tbsp parsley leaves

To use the dressing straight away, blend all the ingredients together in a blender, including the whole parsley leaves. If the dressing is to be stored, blend or shake the other ingredients together. Chop the parsley and stir it into the dressing just before serving.

Yoghurt Herb Dressing

Another low-calorie dressing, avoiding the use of oil.

1 small carton yoghurt, chilled
1 shallot

1 tsp made English mustard
1 tbsp parsley leaves

1   Peel and roughly chop the shallot.
2   Put all the ingredients into a blender, cover and blend at maximum speed until the shallot is finely chopped. Serve chilled.

Blue Cheese Dressing

To serve with green salads, particularly lettuce, endive, chicory or Chinese leaves.

150 ml (¼ pt) olive or other salad
   oil
150 ml (¼ pt) cider vinegar
50 g (2 oz) Danish Blue cheese,
   crumbled

1 tbsp caster sugar
½ tsp paprika
½ tsp salt

Blend all the ingredients together until the cheese disappears and the dressing is cloudy. Store in a screw-topped jar. For a coarse dressing, blend all the other ingredients together, then stir in the crumbled or grated blue cheese.

Greek Oil and Lemon Dressing

The Greeks serve a simple lemon dressing not only on salads, but on cooked green vegetables, which are elevated to a course by themselves. It is delicious on spinach or green beans.

150 ml (¼pt) olive oil at room   1 clove garlic
   temperature   ¼ tsp white pepper
4 tbsp lemon juice

Whisk, beat or blend the ingredients together and allow them to
stand at room temperature for at least 1 hour before serving. The
dressing can be stored in a refrigerator, but should be brought back
to room temperature before serving.

Honey Dressing

Serve this sweet dressing with cabbage and other green salads.

4 tbsp clear honey   300 ml (½pt) olive oil
150 ml (¼pt) white wine vinegar

Put all the ingredients into a blender, cover, and blend at high
speed for 1 minute.

Sweet and Sour Salad Dressing

Especially good with the crispest of salad vegetables, such as white
and red cabbage, and beetroot.

4 tbsp clear honey   1 tsp lemon juice
1 tbsp wine vinegar   a good pinch of mustard powder
8 drops soy sauce   a good pinch of mixed spice

Blend, beat or shake all the ingredients together. Store in a screw-
top jar in the refrigerator, but bring to room temperature before
serving.

Spiced Orange Dressing

This dressing is at its best with a salad containing fruit such as
raisins, sultanas or dates.

4 tbsp vegetable oil   salt
2 tbsp Worcestershire sauce   freshly ground black pepper
1 orange

1   Squeeze the juice and grate the rind of the orange.
2   Blend, whisk or shake the ingredients together.

Cocktail Sauce

Bottled sauces bring together a blend of ingredients it would take
ages to assemble. Use this dressing for shellfish and other fish
cocktails, or for avocado pears.

4 tbsp mayonnaise   *a few drops of Worcestershire*
4 tbsp tomato ketchup   *sauce and Yorkshire Relish*
4 tbsp single cream

Mix all the ingredients together and chill in a covered container in
the refrigerator.

Savoury Sauce

To serve with kebabs, or barbecued meat.

1 small onion   *2 tsp Chop Sauce*
4 gherkins   *1 tsp malt vinegar*
150 ml ($\frac{1}{4}$pt) mayonnaise   *1 tsp Yorkshire Relish*

1   Peel and grate the onion. Finely chop the gherkin.
2   Combine all the ingredients together and chill in a covered
    container for at least 3 hours.

Cider and Raisin Sauce

To serve with grilled gammon, bacon or pork chops.

600 ml (1 pt) dry cider   *1 tbsp water*
50 g (2 oz) seedless raisins   *1 tbsp Yorkshire Relish*
1 tbsp cornflour   *2 tbsp soft dark brown sugar*

1   Pour the cider into a saucepan, add the raisins and bring to the
    boil. Boil until the liquid is reduced by half.
2   Stir the water into the cornflour to make a smooth paste, then
    stir it into the cider mixture.
3   Bring to the boil again, stirring, add the Yorkshire Relish and
    sugar and stir over a low heat until the sugar has melted. Serve
    hot.

Cider and Honey Basting Sauce

Use this to baste kebabs or meat as it grills.

4 tbsp dry cider   *2 tbsp tomato purée*
4 tbsp clear honey   *1 tbsp lemon juice*

Heat all the ingredients together and stir well. Use to baste meat.
Heat remaining sauce and serve hot.

Barbecue Sauce

You don't have to have an outdoor barbecue to enjoy the peppery
sweetness of barbecue sauce. This one goes well with steaks,
gammon or pork chops.

1 medium-sized onion
1 tbsp vegetable oil
1 tbsp flour
150 ml (¼ pt) water
1 tbsp tomato purée

1 tbsp redcurrant jelly
1 tbsp malt vinegar
1 tbsp Worcestershire sauce
10 stuffed green olives

1 Peel and finely chop the onion.
2 Heat the oil in a small pan, fry the onion over moderate heat
   until soft, and stir in the flour. Gradually pour on the water,
   stirring until thickened.
3 Add the tomato purée, redcurrant jelly, vinegar and Worcestershire sauce. Simmer for 10 minutes.
4 Slice the olives thinly and stir into the sauce. Serve hot.

Bitter Orange Sauce

For grilled gammon, bacon or pork chops.

5 tbsp dark chunky marmalade
2 tbsp orange juice
1 tbsp lemon juice

2 tbsp raisins
1 tbsp soft dark brown sugar

Put all the ingredients together in a pan and simmer them gently
for 5 minutes. Garnish the dish, if you like, with fresh orange
slices.

Sauce Base

Save a little time by keeping a basic butter and flour roux mix. All
you need to do is stir in milk or stock for an instant sauce. The roux
will keep in the refrigerator for two weeks.

225 g (8 oz) butter   *225 g (8 oz) flour*

1 Heat the butter in a small pan. Sprinkle on the flour, stirring
   with a wooden spoon until the mixture leaves the sides of the

pan. Cook over a very low heat for 15 minutes, but do not allow the mixture to brown.

2   Cool the roux, then store it in a covered container in the refrigerator.

3   To use the sauce base, measure 3 level tablespoons into a small pan, allow to heat, then gradually pour on 300 ml ($\frac{1}{2}$ pint) milk or stock. Add seasonings and flavouring to choice.

These proportions make a steady pouring sauce. Add half the quantity of liquid to make a thick coating sauce.

Sweet Toppings

So many fast-food puddings, delicious and creamy, are even better with a quick crunchy topping. Whether it is a scattering of toasted coconut on a snowy meringue, a crackling of nutty crumbs on a smooth, fruity ice-cream, or a tanning of golden-brown flakes on a velvet cream, the topping can make the dish.

Nuts must come top of the list, but prepare them in advance: they're fiddly to prepare at the last moment.

Toasted Nuts

Toast blanched almonds on a baking tray at 180 °C (350 °F), Gas 4, and cook them for about 15 minutes, shaking the tray from time to time. Or toast them on a piece of foil in the base of a grill pan, under a medium-to-hot grill. Cool the nuts before storing them in a screw-top jar.

Toast ground hazelnuts in the same way—they are specially good on meringues and mousses. And keep a mini store of toasted coconut for banana, rum or brandy-flavoured puddings.

Chopped walnuts, a good topping in their own right, are even better mixed with buttered crumbs—golden, gooey and chewy all at once.

Walnut Crumble

Bake this mixture one time when you have the oven on, allow it to cool, then crumble it into a jar for safe keeping. Sprinkle on fruit, ice-cream or mousses.

50 g (2 oz) demerara sugar   *100 g (4 oz) butter*
50 g (2 oz) chopped walnuts   *100 g (4 oz) flour*

1   Put all the ingredients in a bowl and mix with a fork until they form coarse crumbs.
2   Spread the crumbs over a non-stick baking tray and bake at 200 °C (400 °F), Gas 6, for 10–12 minutes, until they are golden brown. Leave to cool on the tray, then crumble in your fingers.

Almond Flakes

Cereal flakes and almonds quickly stir into a golden topping for cream puddings, try them with yoghurt mallows.

25 g (1 oz) butter   *50 g (2 oz) chopped almonds*
50 g (2 oz) cornflakes   *50 g (2 oz) granulated sugar*

1   Melt the butter in a small pan and stir in the other ingredients.
2   Remove the pan from the heat, cool, then crumble the flakes in your fingers. Store when cool in a covered container in the refrigerator.

Savoury Toppings

Onion Crumb Topping

You just re-heat this topping in a small pan. A couple of spoonfuls make all the difference to Brussels sprouts, broccoli, cauliflower or courgettes.

1 medium-sized onion   *25 g (1 oz) chopped walnuts*
50 g (2 oz) butter   *salt*
100 g (4 oz) fresh breadcrumbs   *freshly ground black pepper*

1   Peel and finely chop the onion.
2   Heat the butter in a frying-pan and fry the onion until it is soft. Stir in the breadcrumbs and walnuts and season with salt and pepper. Fry them over a medium heat until the crumbs are golden and dry.
3   Leave the crumbs in the pan to cool, then break them up with a fork. Store in a covered container in the refrigerator.

Cheesy Crumb Topping

A hint of garlic behind the cheese—a garnish to try with courgettes, broccoli and cauliflower.

1 medium-sized onion   *40 g (1½ oz) butter*
1 clove garlic   *100 g (4 oz) fresh breadcrumbs*
50 g (2 oz) cheese   *salt and paprika*

1   Peel and finely chop the onion. Peel and crush the garlic. Grate the cheese.
2   Heat the butter in a frying-pan and fry the onion and garlic for 4–5 minutes over medium heat. Stir in the breadcrumbs and cook until they are nearly dry. Stir in the grated cheese, season with salt and paprika and allow the cheese just to melt. Cool in the pan.
3   Crumble up the topping and store it in a covered container in the refrigerator.

Croûtons

Croûtons are usually served with soups, nice and bitey, on top of a smooth broth. Very tiny ones make a super garnish for green vegetables.

4 1-cm (½-in) slices white bread   *2 tsp dried parsley, or 1 tbsp celery*
1 large clove garlic (optional)   *seed (see method)*
oil or fat for frying

1   Cut the crusts from the bread. Cut the bread into 1-cm (½-in) cubes for soup, 0·5-cm (¼-in) cubes to garnish vegetables.
2   For garlic croûtons, peel and crush the garlic.
3   Heat the oil or fat in a frying-pan. Fry the garlic if used. When the fat is just smoking, toss in the bread cubes and fry them, turning them once, until they are mid-brown on both sides.
4   Remove them with a draining spoon and dry them on crumpled kitchen paper.
5   Put the dried parsley in a bag and toss the croûtons in it. When they are cool, put them in a screw-top jar.

As an alternative, toss the croûtons in a bag with the celery seed. These are delicious scattered on cauliflower—or, indeed, on braised celery.

Flavoured Sugars

Puddings and baked goods made with herb-flavoured sugars—it's an old trick, and easy as pie to copy.

Keep caster or granulated sugar in several screw-top jars and give each one its own personality.

Wash and dry a sprig of rosemary, bay leaves, lavender (before the flowers open) and laurel. Put the herbs each in a jar, fill nearly to the brim with sugar, cover, and shake occasionally. Put a couple of sticks of cinnamon in another jar. A vanilla pod in another jar. When a recipe recommends that you use 'vanilla sugar', this is what it means. And you can produce it, or any of these variations, in two shakes.

Index